Methods of Ethical Analysis

Methods of Ethical Analysis

Between Theology, History, and Literature

Nimi Wariboko

WIPF & STOCK · Eugene, Oregon

METHODS OF ETHICAL ANALYSIS
Between Theology, History, and Literature

Copyright © 2013 Nimi Wariboko. All rights reserved. Except for brief quotations in critical publications or reviews, no part of this book may be reproduced in any manner without prior written permission from the publisher. Write: Permissions, Wipf and Stock Publishers, 199 W. 8th Ave., Suite 3, Eugene, OR 97401.

Wipf & Stock
An Imprint of Wipf and Stock Publishers
199 W. 8th Ave., Suite 3
Eugene, OR 97401
www.wipfandstock.com

ISBN 13: 978-1-62564-011-6
Manufactured in the U.S.A.

To a dear friend, General Owoye Andrew Azazi,
who passed away in December 2012.

Contents

Acknowledgments ix

Introduction 1

Chapter 1 Ethical Methodology: Between Public Theology and Public Policy 19

Chapter 2 Jeffrey Stout's Theory of Public Reason 36

Chapter 3 Max Stackhouse: Globalization and Theology of History 63

Chapter 4 Emergence and "Science of Ethos": Toward a Tillichian Ethical Framework 80

Chapter 5 The Evasion of Ethics: Peter Paris Feels the Spirituals 103

Chapter 6 Literature and Ethics: Learning from Martha Nussbaum 126

Chapter 7 Conclusion: Ethics of Methodology 141

Bibliography 153
Subject Index 159
Name Index 163

ACKNOWLEDGMENTS

I WOULD LIKE TO thank Professor Amos Yong of Regent University for his comments on the introduction and chapter 7. Nancy Shoptaw served as superb copyeditor, ferreting out errors with excellence and smoothing the flow of language. I also thank Christian Amondson, Jim Tedrick, and Diane Farley at Wipf and Stock Publishers.

I gratefully acknowledge permission to reprint three essays published elsewhere. Chapter 1 published as "Ethical Methodology: Between Public Theology and Public Policy." *Journal of Religion and Business Ethics* 1, no. 1 (Winter 2010). Chapter 4 appeared earlier as "Emergence and 'Science of Ethos:' Toward a Tillichian Ethical Framework." *Theology and Science* 7, no. 2 (May 2009) 189–206. Copyright 2009 by Taylor and Francis. All rights reserved. Reprinted with the permission of Taylor and Francis Ltd. Finally, chapter 5 appeared as "The Evasion of Ethics: Peter Paris feels the Spirituals." *Toronto Journal of Theology*, 27, no. 2 (2011) 215–33.

Introduction

THIS BOOK IS A tutorial in ethical analysis and reasoning. Master of divinity students will be brought into the finer points of ethical analysis, of mastering the ins and outs of ethical methodology, by immersing themselves in critical social-ethical analyses of prominent scholars in the American academy. Students will be guided toward how to develop their own voice in social issues, hone their capability in social analysis, and critically engage the social sciences, history, philosophy, and literature as they embark on ethical analyses. There is no single way of teaching the methodology of social ethics and no single theory of ethics that satisfies all, therefore ethics and its methodology are better understood by enabling students to view the field through multiple "windows." Simultaneously they will learn to view social reality from different perspectives. The seven chapters of this book explore the different ways American ethicists have interrogated their nation's moral systems or crafted methods for understanding them.

The very first chapter is a distillation of what I believe is the most prevalent methodology of social ethics in the American academy. It paints a portrait of ethical methodology in the academy. This portrait of ethical methodology in the academy serves as a frame or space through which the thoughts of the five scholars in the remaining chapters are seen. In addition, the chapter provides a lens through which to see their orientations and to appropriate their perspectives.

Chapters 2–6 investigate the work of five scholars: Jeffrey Stout, Max Stackhouse, Paul Tillich, Peter Paris, and Martha Nussbaum as exemplars of ethical methodology. In choosing these ethicists/theologians from a long list of well deserving scholars, I make no claims that they are the single most important ones to study. For our purposes, they represent five distinctive approaches to doing ethics and are representatives of different schools of thought. They were chosen also for the perspectives they bring on different social issues, trends, and events of our times. Indeed their works not only elucidate social issues, they also develop frameworks, procedures, and protocols for navigating and appreciating the diversity of voices, perspectives, experiences, and the kinds of knowledge that stake claims in the public square.

Above all, they were chosen because of the fundamentally different issues of ethical methodology they bring to the field and the public square. Each ethicist challenges students or scholars to examine how they interpret reality and the methods they bring to such an exercise. Thus, the works of these five scholars are part of an ongoing dialogue on methodology.

Some words of caution are in order at this juncture. None of the five scholars set out explicitly to write on ethical methodology. They had other tasks in mind, and whatever "methodology" I have culled from their works is based on my own reading and my interest in showing seminary students how every ethical analysis supervenes on or provides a window on methodology.

One other thread that holds these five scholars together is that their works demonstrate how ethical reasoning is not a form of scientific understanding. Each articulates different aspects of a coherent picture of ethical deliberation. Each is concerned with articulating the notion of the good human functioning that dynamically perfects or completes human life in a community.

To start, Jeffrey Stout examines the nature of public reason that guides ethical deliberation and moral judgment in a democratic public domain. Max Stackhouse argues that to understand globalization we must describe it with the concreteness of historical details, missing nothing of its Christian-spiritual shading and relevance. By this move, Stackhouse is not reducing ethics to history or historiography, but asking us to see ethics as a high type of vision of a particular trajectory of Christian narrative or as meeting of the new of today's globalization with the responsiveness and imagination of the prophets of New Jerusalem. The interpretation of Paul Tillich's ethics via the lens of emergence shows that the subtleties of complex ethical situations suggest we ought to reject calculative, systematic scientific understanding as the best method of ethical reasoning. The chapter on Peter Paris explicitly interprets his work from the perspective of the elimination of racism in the United States as necessary for good human functioning of all persons. Martha Nussbaum, working from an Aristotelian conception of the ethical, offers an alternative "scientific understanding" of ethical reasoning, the *perceptive equilibrium*. This is "an equilibrium in which concrete perceptions 'hang beautifully together,' both with one another and with agent's general principles; an equilibrium that is always ready to reconstitute itself in response to the new."[1]

The thoughts of these five scholars in chapters 2-6 are arranged in two parts. In the first part I group together the more philosophic/theological (abstract and generalized) approaches to ethical methodology. This means approaches to ethical methodology that are not to specific social issues or social location but can be applied to any issue or location that is at stake. Here I start with Stout with a generalized American focus on public reason; moving to Stackhouse in chapter 3 with a global focus on the providential movement of history, and ending with Tillich (chapter 4) on his global philosophic (metaphysics) argument and its connection to science of emergence. These three philosophic-theological arguments, as good as they, are not useful for all things and they tell us only half of the story. We need to complement them with more concrete methodological options. For the ethical methodology that I have laid out in chapter 1 combines both philosophical-theological and concrete-particular approaches to ethics. The last two of the five chapters illustrate what the ethical methodology looks like in particular, concrete moral contexts. The first of these two chapters examines the concrete context of racism in the United States. The other shows how novelist's attention to the particular and concrete enriches our understanding of the vision of the ethical methodology. In part two I bring together the works of Paris and Nussbaum in chapters 5 and 6 respectively. Paris reveals the relevance of the particular African-American narrative context and the experience of racism in the study of ethics in the United States. From Nussbaum we will learn the importance of particular literary approaches to ethics. This sequence is informed by the need to start the learning process from the very philosophical issues of public reason, to encompassing concerns of theology of history, to the benefits of multidisciplinary perspectives that science brings to social ethics, to the contextual issues of racism in the United States, and finally literature as particular aid to public reasoning in particular, concrete situations.[2]

These five chapters provide a coherent trajectory of arguments that funds pluralistic ethical methodology for public policy in the United States.

1. Nussbaum, *Love's Knowledge*, 182–83.
2. I need to add that the characterization of the chapters as either abstract or concrete does not mean that theoretical and practical elements are not present in each of them. The elements are fused in all the chapters, as I will argue below. The characterization I have given here is meant to only indicate the general, predominant tendency in each of them.

Read together, the five chapters capture the seriousness of formulating an ethical method (with its intrinsically pluralist presuppositions) for the public square, not a set of technical issues in morality or rhetorical strategy, but as a boundary that secures *truths* in a democratic society and for the existential survival of the particular American way of life. The recognition of truths in a democratic society and the process of learning to appropriate them for public policies will always demand that we listen to the many voices, "many tongues" and examine multiple perspectives on social issues in our communities.

Though this book is about methodology rather than a traditional subject of social ethics or any particular point of theology, it offers relevantly multiple perspectives on socio-economic issues that have preoccupied both theologians and ethicists. This is so because this book is not about a methodology conjured up in the arid, thin air of rootless thought; it is not a metatheory floating above the diversity of concrete studies. The methodology laid out here developed out of the analysis of major social issues of the twenty-first century. So we are learning about the methodology of social ethics as we explore the issues of theology and public policy, public reason and democratic tradition, globalization and global civil society, biology of emergence and ethics, racism and African-American thought, and literature and moral imagination. The selection of these topics does not follow any pattern that may be described as history of ideas. To say this, however, is to not provide an excuse, but to use differences and discontinuities to explore different aspects of ethical methodology. It is also to point to the key roles played by theological perspectives, social analysis, historical interpretation, analysis of oppression and discrimination, literary imagination, and philosophy in contemporary ethical analysis and reasoning.

The methodology of this book is a set of fruits plucked from trees of analysis planted in the garden of concrete life issues. It is a plucking rather than a new planting because each of the essays is crafted to show not only how a particular subject matter is treated, but even more importantly, dissects the method behind the analysis that sustains the treatment. Every chapter is an exemplar of the overall methodology put forward by this book. Each gives us an understanding of the fundamental issues of the methodology and a clear direction of thought as to how social ethics is useful in understanding and transforming reality.

There are two elements running through chapters 2–6: a perceptive view of the currents of the present, that is, the conceptual expression of

Introduction

reality, the rigorous treatment of a subject matter, which I will designate as thought element. Then there is the practical element, which consists of the methods of ethical analysis. This fusion of the two elements in each of the chapters expresses a distinct characteristic, namely that the treatment of an ethical or theological matter has value only as they set forth or affect a methodological outlook. In this union, the treatment of theological-ethical (philosophical) issues aims at that which is meaningful for the development of a methodology, a way of approaching the study of social issues. With this approach, ethical analysis is a methodology and ethical methodology is an analysis. This is not an afterthought. Right from the beginning I have written the essays as part of one integrative work. This is a thoughtful approach designed to build students' competence on ethical methodology around analysis of critical social issues.

This book has created mixtures of methodological practices and it may appear difficult for readers who are not approaching it to learn how to do ethical analysis to see the structure of the forest as a whole. What is the overall "wholeness" of the book if one is to avoid the accusation of creating methodological practices for their own sake? In one sense, we should provide one synoptic map even though what matters for the students' learning is something that necessarily involves a constellation of methodological practices. In another sense, doing this defeats the purpose of the book. The book is about showing different ways of doing ethics, highlighting a kind of methodological pluralism. To reduce or force all the methodological practices into one mold or central view does violence to the premise of the book. Whether this kind of central view is presented as singleness (this preferred method against all others) or as totality (this is all there is to a good ethical methodology) that rejects all other methodologies as not valid. But I want students to use any of the five methodologies to discover and amplify their own voices without obliterating others or putting their own chosen methodology into the category of "universal truth." These are individual voices that are owned but are not afraid to include echoes of many voices and are open to resonate with others.

This attempt to refuse the crafting of a central dominant view that puts all the five methodological practices on a kind of totalizing synoptic map should not be construed to mean that each of the methodologies is differentiated and self-enclosed. In the work of an experienced ethicist each method as a non-self-enclosed approach to social issues works in communion with the other methods to a lesser or greater degree. All I want is for MDiv students to develop the competence and perspective that will give their own methodologies this kind of mutually appreciative welcomed generosity.

This long explanation of the importance of each student to insert her own voice in the differential scholarly practice that conjoins methods and contents without stepping outside a recognizable methodology to do so is the "structure of the forest as a whole" in the first place. In her engagement with the different methodologies the MDiv student will develop her own different voice. If ethics matters, then difference must matter in methodology as well. If we have difference we have ethics (having alternative, doing something new) in pluralistic societies. If we do not we will either have just one dominant good and how to present or impose it on others for public policy or an undifferentiated existence. The forms of social existence constructed by pluralistic ethos are meant to be differential rather than identitarian. This book attempts to relate the difference in methodology and perspective to difference in identity, focal point of analysis, or projects of persuasion. Difference matters ultimately because pluralism matters. Pluralism is an acknowledged *consocial* stance and exercise of separation and interdependencies in social existence. It is a conscious exercise in defining and fostering human flourishing in non-unitary communities.

If we affirmed identity and difference in this kind of particularity, as noted above, what does it mean for the student to speak in her own voice? It is to speak out of the center of a methodology that is itself serious about pluralism. Getting this point across to MDiv students is the whole purpose, the synoptic intent, of the book.

Public Theology: Common Good and Pentecost

Having said all this, I want to add that not all theologians (such as those in the Radical Orthodox and Postliberal theology movements) in the United States might want to follow this kind of reasoning. Scholars outside these movements as well as those within, like Stanley Hauerwas, talk about the church as a social ethic, a "resident alien" providing an alternative ethics to the general society.[3] Although Hauerwas expects the church to witness to the God found in the life, death, and resurrection of Jesus Christ, Catholic

---

3. "Put starkly, the first social ethical task of the church is to be the church—the servant community.... As such the church does not have a social ethic; the church is a social ethic." Hauerwas, *Peaceable Kingdom*, 99.

theologian Lisa Sowle Cahill argues that Hauerwas's "focus is not on Jesus's inclusive ministry of the reign of God, nor on the power of the resurrection to overcome suffering and enable socially transformative communities. He does not see a new way available within those communities, but it consists in maintaining fidelity to demanding internal ideals, while expecting incomprehension and rejection by the world outside the church."[4]

Thus, Hauerwas and his followers are ill suited for the kind of ethical methodology or public theology I am advocating in this book. Their own path to ethics is not geared to engage with the democratic project of nation-building, to connecting the Christian conceptions of God (ultimate concern) and salvation to the real-life social issues and concrete problems of social coexistence. Given the notion of church as ethics, which focuses on "soulcraft" at the expense of "statecraft" as a proper direction of Christian ethics, theologians like Hauerwas will not encourage the teaching of a methodology for public theology, if I understand them well.[5] In its focus, this book does not offer all the important approaches to ethical reasoning or ethics *per se*; it is only about crafting a methodology for public theology or social ethics, for ethicists' engagement with public policy or public reasoning in pluralistic societies. Public theology is a viable and sustainable path to the promises of Christian ethics, but not because there is something supremely unique about it. What it has going for it is that it summons the right combination of critique and transformation, and the vision of a flourishing commons to support all of God's children. Besides, it has the non-exclusionary tendency to accommodate all in equal terms under the tent of the common good.

While I do not reject the stance of Hauerwas and his followers, I am willing to enlarge my understanding of ethics to include participation in the just and democratic process of nation-building. My decision to extend the purview of Christian ethics to encompass public theology is based on the principles that (a) ethicists should participate in the ongoing intellectual and practical definition and determination of the common good of their societies, and (b) they should contribute to the collective, improvisatory process of figuring out how to realize the common good in differences. These two principles have given limits and license to my discourse on ethical methodology.

---

4. Cahill, "Theological Ethics," 379.

5. For an admirable discussion of politics-as-statecraft and politics-as-soulcraft, see Burroughs, "Christianity, Politics, and the Predicament of Evil."

Methods of Ethical Analysis

What is the specific notion of the common good that guides this book and how does it relate to differences in the public square? What are the demands it makes on ethical methodology? I must state from the outset that my interpretation (an immanent understanding) of common good is just one among many. It is possible to propose other interpretations that might work well with the constructive proposal of ethical methodology in this book. In developing one here, my interest is not to enter into the thicket of debates over the "true" conceptuality of the common good. It is, more precisely, to further develop our understanding of the ethical methodology I am advancing.

The common good of any society is truly common only when it is in immanent relation with all goods in that society. The existence of a common good in a society means that for each and every one in that community the cause and effect of all goods belong to the same plane.[6] The distinction between goods (such as relations of cause and effect, prior and consequent) is precluded insofar as the common good at the collective level refuses two or multiple categories of goods, two uncommon planes of goods or priority.[7] No groups, classes, or persons stand in relation of transcendence to another even as their positions or preferences are distinguishable. All positions, preferences, and distinctions therefore are preserved in immanent relation. The common good is that good the realization of which demands that every good (of a class, group, race, person) affects others as much as others are affected by it.[8]

The common good is the site of public policy's origin and public policy undoing. The common good is not bound by public policy, juridical norms, or sectional values and so may decide exceptions to them. This understanding of the common good relies on a philosophical-theological underpinning, on a reading of the event of Pentecost in Acts 2. Pentecost represents an expression of a certain intensity of God's presence in the midst of Christ's disciples after the resurrection. The wind that blew suddenly, touching everyone, and the tongues of fire that accompanied it is a realization of *desire*, an intensive communicative and collaborative interaction of desires, to use French philosopher Gilles Deleuze's term. Pentecost

---

6. The concept of the common good as developed in this book is indebted to Daniel Barber's interpretation of immanence. I have followed his interpretation to creatively fashion a fresh conceptuality of common good on the pivot of immanence. See Barber, *On Diaspora*.

7. Collective here means a sharing and not a fusion or communion.

8. This concept of the common good is further developed in chapter 7.

is an intensification of the human capacity to act, the power of acting in certain ways; the reign of God is recognized as the sovereignty of decentering of spaces with formulatable boundaries, as a mode of bonding, as a mode of existence of other-regarding love with unformulatable boundaries.

Pentecost is an intensification of desire that is the condition for the production of the new: a straining into the *novum*, it is generative of hope of new possibilities. It is the kind of desire that "endlessly creates new connections with others, embraces difference, and fosters a proliferation of relations between fluxes of desire. As such desire is the power of collaboration and sociality, and to such power Deleuze gives the name 'love' and 'joy,' while the sociality he equates with playing and dancing."[9]

This kind of desire is connected with the immanent presence and the communion-creating presence of the Holy Spirit and constitutes a political question. What can I do or what am I capable of doing to extend the relationality of the Spirit or that is the Spirit?[10] With the event of Pentecost, Christ's disciples had a stake in investing in a world that will express—not repress or thwart—their desire for the relationality of the Spirit and will create an interest in the Spirit. They had an interest in organizing and assembling the desire of the Spirit as part of the infrastructure of the world.

Let us turn to the theological aspects of Acts 2, the story of the manifestation/immanence of the Spirit for the common good. The gifts of language and fire were given to each person for the profit of *all*. The gifts were given to bring diversity among the disciples and to benefit the whole of the emerging community. The Spirit is a common blessing to all, for the manifestation of the common good as Paul reminds us in 1 Corinthians 12:7, but it alights differently, in diverse forms among the disciples. One does not possess the Holy Spirit as one's own exclusive property nor all of the Spirit's gifts, potentialities and actualizations. One possesses a gift or gifts of the Spirit, and so becomes a believer with distinctive and particular gifts. So the manifestation of the common good "is achieved in ways that are not common to all."[11]

Pentecost is relationality, marked by diversity, inclusiveness, invitation, equity, and new relationship-making power. On the day of Pentecost, the Holy Spirit united the disciples and three thousand others into a people/multitude or a new and joyful community, but each person remained

---

9. Bell, *Economy of Desire*, 44.
10. See Loder, *Logic of the Spirit*; Loder and Neidhardt, *Knight's Move*.
11. Norton, "Pentecost," 397.

singular and linguistic difference marked the whole group. The disciples were all touched by the fire and sent out into the world by God's spirit to spread the word and establish an egalitarian community, a belongingness of equals before the Lord. Pentecost represents God's action of selecting the multitude, the people as the sovereign body on earth, bypassing the preselected, wellborn or well-endowed, to do his work. The pentecostal fire fell not on the priests, but on the people. The people were empowered to become the voice of God and to express God's will in favor of a society's privileged few who can hand down strategies and stratagems, solutions and statutes, and results and rankings to others in the name of God. This alternative sovereignty to the authoritarian powers of the day (secular and ecclesiastical) was marked from its inception by equality, solidarity, and unity-in-difference. Political theorist Anne Norton says:

> At the moment in which they recognize themselves as the *demos*, the people are united by the *heilege geist*, that common mind and spirit that realizes itself in language, more precisely in linguistic difference. The people are united, they are one, but they remain singular, each equal to the others, all to be sent into the world of equals, undistinguished by birth, power of wealth. They are united in friendship, to broaden ties of unity and communality. They are touched by fire.
> Their work is in language and through language: not one language but in the diverse forms that language takes. They are all to speak, to write, to bear witness; each is to do so in a particular language, a particular tongue.[12]

Norton made this observation in the course of her defense of Carl Schmitt's less known alternative theory of democratic sovereignty based on God's empowerment of the people on the day of Pentecost. If Schmitt's famous theory of sovereignty (the couple of "sovereign is the one who decides on the exception" and the foundation of politics in friend-enemy distinction) is based on the secularization of the incarnation, then, she argues, "the recognition of sovereignty in the people is a secular Pentecost."[13]

The being-together of the new expanded community of disciples was founded on friendship and language, not on violence, not on friend-enemy distinction, and not on national or racial difference.[14] On the day of Pente-

---

12. Norton, "Pentecost," 393–94; italics in the original.
13. Ibid., 393.
14. Lest I be misconstrued, let me add that the Holy Spirit is the primary source of

Introduction

cost language was both the unifying medium of the immanent community and its extension to include the other, and the distinguishing marker of the persons/groups in the commons. Diverse tongues, each person speaking to others and being understood, became the symbol of the interplay between likeness and difference. The combination of likeness and difference, exemplified by language on that fateful day in Jerusalem, is essential for the flourishing of a commons and for the self-determination of its component parts. "Language is a human capacity, but it appears in wildly diverse forms among human beings. One does not learn language, one learns a language, and so becomes human in a distinctive and particular manner. That which is common to all is achieved only in ways that are not common to all."[15]

This character of language ("that which is common to all is achieved only in ways that are not common to all") reflects immanence as the nature of the common good, as we will demonstrate in chapter 7. The common good of any community is common to all its members, but it is not immanent to something, be it even something that is common to all, something that permeates the whole community, if the very something is unaffected by immanent relation. If we are not to deny the immanence of the common good or common good as immanence, we have to accept that the common good is immanent to itself; the common good is common to itself.

To understand the common good in this way, for the purpose of crafting a public policy in a pluralistic society, demands the kind of ethical methodology we are advocating in this book. If one's policy proposal is to be successful and be democratically received in the pluralistic public square, a commons of equals acting in freedom, one needs a methodological language that speaks with others, embraces differences, celebrates multiplicity, and recognizes the sameness of the common good.

This book is about enabling Master of Divinity students to master the language with which to communicate in the public square, to speak in their own voices and in the same vein allow others to speak in their own voices. In the public square, persons, groups, nomads, or multitude speak in many tongues, a secular Pentecost of many voices, driven by interpretations (translations) of the same common good. It is from the symphonic cacophony of voices that the (translated) common good emerges. The many tongues of the day of Pentecost did not prevent the will of God from being expressed in a Jerusalem square in the first century. Similarly, the many

---

their communal strength.

15. Norton, "Pentecost," 397.

voices of the public square (Boston Common) of the twenty-first century will not forestall the expression of the common good, even as it relates to a contested public policy. The making of public policy in a pluralistic society should never rest on blindness to what distinguishes persons or groups in a commons, but rather it must maintain a clear-sighted focus on the common good. The common good, as we will argue in chapter 7, is discernible only in ways that have not been reduced to one.

And here we want to add that the common good in a democratic pluralistic society is not discernible apart from a daily engagement with the paradox of people and multitude, the paradox of politics. Norton's analogy of language (commonality and singularity) as applied to the day of Pentecost (or the analogizing of the immanence of the Spirit to language) introduces the paradox of people and multitude. The gift of language unifies the disciples and their listeners into a people as well as renders them a multitude. Being touched and empowered by the same Spirit is a unifying experience, but each person is separated from the other by a specific tongue. The quotidian problem becomes how to shape and reshape the multitude into a people. (This is a problem that is particularly acute in Pentecostalism. Pentecostals may be united by the Spirit, but they are divided by personally claimed individual access to spiritual gifts: they disavow Rousseau's lawgiver, whether charlatan or authentic.) As American political theorist Bonnie Honig informs us, the agonistic struggle to (re)shape the multitude to a people is the very character (or the endemic problem) of democratic politics. She states: "The irresolvable paradox of politics commits us to a view of the people, democratic actors and subjects, as also always a multitude. The paradox of politics posits democracy as always embedded in the problem of origins and survival: how to (re)shape a multitude into a people, daily."[16]

In a certain sense our ethical methodology can be considered as part of the quotidian attempt to (re)shape the multitudinous voices in the public square into a collective will for just public policies. Albeit, the method does not guarantee that the general will would be free from the impurities of the will of all or that the multitude will be a people. The ethical methodology I am advancing in this book provides a passage—or at least the markings of one—from the passion-inducing good drama of the immanence of Spirit (or any kind of revolutionary fervor) to the popular-sovereign politics and everyday task of good self-governance.

16. Honig, *Emergency Politics*, xvii.

Introduction

What do we hope to get as we make our way through this passage? "Here, we get neither deliberation nor decision as such; we get politics, in which plural and contending parties make claims in the name of public goods and seek support from various constituencies and wherein the legitimacy of outcomes is always contestable."[17] This agonistic struggle suggests another paradox. The common good for which our ethical methodology works (presupposes) and to which it appeals (promises) may not yet exist. Yet it is our duty to hope, without which we can generate neither the power nor the desire to work, act dutifully, for the common good.

Outline of Chapters

Apart from chapters 1 and 7, every chapter begins with an "Opening Word." This section is different from the chapter's introduction. In the opening-word section of chapters 2 to 6, I will explain how the ideas of chapter 1 ("Ethical Methodology: Between Theology and Public Policy") echo in the work of the scholar under study, and how the chapter's analysis and presentation reinforce the ideas of chapter 1. Not that teachers and students cannot figure this out by themselves, but I take this approach because I want the book to be as classroom-friendly as possible. The placement of an "opening word" at the beginning of each chapter is also geared toward easy review and a building up of the competence of the students on an ongoing basis. On turning to a new chapter, I want students to quickly understand how his or her competence is built up layer by layer, fold by fold. Here a little and there a little. Gaining confidence and competence is all about repetition and reinforcement of lessons learned!

Chapter 1 develops an explicit procedural method of ethical analysis relevant to public policy decision-making. The chapter proposes an ethical methodology as a form of discourse, a meta-ethical method showing how themes, concerns, and insights of public theology can be systematically organized into practical policy arguments. A robust "mechanics" is provided to aid students to prepare ethical analyses for public policies.

In this chapter, I argue for the irreducible importance of theological perspectives, social analysis, historical interpretation, analysis of oppression and discrimination, literary imagination, and philosophy in ethical analysis and reasoning. Each of the subsequent five chapters not only shows how different scholars use these sources to illuminate social problems and

17. Ibid., 37.

ethical thinking, but they also represent subtle variations, a deepening and broadening of the overall architecture of ethical methodology in chapter 1.

The ethical methodology discussed in chapter 1 represents a commitment to a public exchange of reasons in democratic pluralistic communities. In such communities there are (or ought to be) standards for accepting reasons or claims for public policy. What are these standards in the United States? Or how can we formulate and evaluate them? The demand to grapple with these kinds of pertinent questions that must inform the ethical methodology, which we have developed in chapter 1, drives us to the work of Jeffrey Stout, religious ethicist and philosopher at Princeton University. Stout is concerned with the standard of public debate or justified reason. According to him, one of the purposes of moral theory or ethics is to develop a standard for public evaluation or discourse that can either serve to adjudicate or focus conflicting viewpoints. Such is a standard we can use to regulate, revise, and correct our moral judgment or critique the views of others. The standard for accepting a reason as justified is that of a claim that is justified in the sense that no relevant reasons for doubting it remain standing within a given discursive context.

How citizens engage with reason in the public domain is often informed by their faith tradition and their interpretation of the socio-economic trends as informed by their theologies and dominant religious worldview. Take, for instance, debates about globalization. They are not only informed by economic and technological benefits to individuals and nation-states, but also by an eschatological (religious) view of history. In chapter 3, I explicate Max Stackhouse's theology of history as an aspect of his theological ethics. His theology of history is the church (*ecclesia*) interpreted in terms of the spiritual impulses of history, the dynamics of globalization, and the movement toward the *New Jerusalem,* an urban, cosmopolitan civilization, a global civil society. The church, as the "mother" of a new and decisive kind of social institution beyond kinship, class, and state, is the turning point in history and it is that which can potentially lead history to its fulfillment, to the New Jerusalem. Globalization is a providential process that is leading humanity to the global civil society, to the New Jerusalem. In this journey, he argues, the church is the originary image of globalization's future. The role of public theology (drawing its values and orientation principally from the Judeo-Christian worldview) is to define the proper ethos for the emerging global civilization.

Introduction

The methodological lesson of this chapter is that Stackhouse shows us how to bring philosophy of history and ethics together in our analyses of social issues. Ethics and its methodology, he believes, must be situated or undergirded by the theological contemplation of the panorama of history. His philosophy of history provides the systematic orientation to his ethics in general and to special studies on select subject matters.

From international issues of globalization and global civil society, the book moves to science and ethics, increasing our knowledge of the general theoretical approach to ethical methodology. Chapter 4 offers an ethical framework informed by *emergence*. Specifically, the chapter examines how the biology of emergence is likely to influence not only methodology, but also the nature of ethical thought. Here I invite Paul Tillich as conversation partner to aid me in exploring the key intersections of ethics, biology, and the philosophy of emergence. Using Tillich's notion of ethics as "science of ethos" or "science of culture" this chapter attempts to work out some of the ethical implications of emergence. The implications are brought to light in an ethical framework that not only traces and clarifies the lure of the mystery at work in the culturally-creative functions of persons and social groups, but also shows how the creative functions of human life can express the unconditional eros of serendipitous creativity.

From the abstract philosophical-theological treatise and international issues of ethical thinking, the book moves to the concrete, domestic issue of racism and the kind of methodology that works to expose it in American society. Chapter 5 shows students how the commitment of African Americans to the eradication of racism nudges many of them to "evade" the establishment's definition of the subject matter of and approach to social ethics in the academy. Peter Paris is an exemplary scholar in this regard.

This chapter provides not only a systematic account of Peter Paris's theology and ethics, but also a critical interpretation of his thought. Racism is identified as the major problem that has engaged Paris's academic career and at the same time the theological-ethical methodology he has developed to understand and explain it. He has been able to do all of this in ways that *evade* and challenge the American theological enterprise.

The primary theme of Paris's work is evading epistemology-centered ethics, exposing racism and injustice, and accenting the transformation of the structures of domination and subordination in the light of an ethical ideal, which is usually the thwarting of evil or actualization of human potentialities. In doing this, he converts ethics into a positive science of social critique and a cultural investigation of the social crises of the United States.

The importance of this chapter goes beyond interpreting Paris's thought, as it will be useful to scholars teaching ethics in general and African-American ethics in particular. Paris's evasion of ethics is rooted in the black religious tradition of ethical critique of American society in order to expose its moral limits and remind it of its blindnesses, as W. E. B. Du Bois informed us. The chapter, in also locating the thought of Paris in the deep ethos that informed the *spirituals*, reveals another major dimension of the African-American ethical scholarship. Most importantly, by carefully discussing the ethical methodology of Paris in particular, this chapter clarifies that of African-American ethicists in general.

A question suggests itself at this juncture in the study: How can we move from the practical issues of crafting methodology to the practical matters of conscientizing the heart, which is also important for ethical praxis? Can a teacher who instructs students or aspiring ethicists on methodology in the same breath tug at their heart, fire their creative and moral imagination? Is there a way, a method to teach ethics and its methodology that can capture the moral imagination of students and raise their social consciousness? It was Aristotle who taught us long ago that one of the best ways to teach ethics is to use literature as a valuable tool toward developing moral imagination. Lionel Trilling states this well: "I spoke of the novel as an especially useful agent of the moral imagination, as the literary form which most directly reveals to us the complexity, the difficulty, and the interest of life in society, and best instructs us in our human variety and contradiction."[18]

Novels, tragic dramas, and other genres have the capacity to help readers identify with fictional characters in ways that show possibilities and potential vulnerabilities for themselves. This kind of empathetic identification is important for good ethical practice in today's diverse and pluralistic communities. Thus, the penultimate chapter of this book explores literature and ethics. Narrative works of art (such as Greek tragedies, modern novels, drama, poems, and films) are important for developing the human self-understanding critical for embodying certain religious and theological ideals. Good ethical conception and practice often demand that we see things from others' points of view. Great novels, plays, poems, and films are

---

18. Trilling, *Moral Obligation*, 510.

good at helping us to reach empathetic perceptions of particular people and situations by involving our intellect and emotion.

Chapter 6 will explore the connections between literature and ethics: the relationship between creative imagination and moral imagination; the nature of moral attention and moral vision; the role of context-specific judging in ethical decisions. The chapter will help students to deepen and broaden their ethical understanding in ways that involve and give priority to compassion, *similar possibilities and vulnerabilities*, and eudaimonistic judgment, rather than abstract general principles. The chapter relies on the thought of philosopher Martha Nussbaum to help students develop the methodological competence relevant for the use of moral imagination and narrative works of art in ethical reasoning.

It is obvious from the above descriptions of the various chapters that this book is not merely about methodology, but about some of the most engaging ethical discourses in the current American academy. Its strength is that it seamlessly marries methodological issues and substantive, practical subject matters to produce a pedagogical form of ethical discourse. Students will learn prevailing, cutting-edge methods of ethical reasoning and philosophizing by being engaged in concrete, relevant studies of social issues as seen through the eyes of some of today's prominent thinkers in the United States. Each of the ethicists opens and then pushes a critical school of thought.

A study of Jeffery Stout in chapter 2 will introduce students to the nature of free public exchange of reasons, which starts from sentiments and religious premises. Stout shows us how the student can acquire "the point of view of a citizen," a necessary equipment for moral judgment in a democratic public domain. We will also learn the importance of the tradition of exchanging reason for the survival of any pluralistic democracy. Max Stackhouse in chapter 3 offers insight on how to theologically interpret globalization. Chapter 4 introduces us to the biology of emergence and its implications for ethical reasoning. In this foray into science and theology, we adopt Paul Tillich as guide. Then in chapter 5, we will study the vexing issue of racism in the United States. Finally, with Martha Nussbaum in chapter 6, we will learn and evaluate the role of literature in shaping public reason and in the education of citizens in pluralistic democracies. In all five chapters we gain crucial insights into the variegated nature of the ethical project that sustains social justice and human flourishing in democratic pluralism.

The Historical and Current Impetus for this Book

I started working on this book in the fall semester of 2007. Right from the beginning my plan was to test all chapters with my master of divinity and doctor of ministry students at Andover Newton Theological School. Between the fall of 2007 and spring of 2012 I have used the various chapter-manuscripts multiple times in six different courses: Introduction to Christian Ethics, Theology and Ethics of Globalization, African-American Politics and Ethics, World Christianity, Theology and Social Theory of Paul Tillich, and Literature and Ethics. I have rewritten them several times based on students' reactions to them and their usefulness in the classroom.

In order to ensure that they meet the highest standards of scholarship, I decided to send a good number of them to academic journals. Three of the chapters have been published in the *Toronto Journal of Theology*, *Theology and Science*, and *Journal of Religion and Business Ethics*. Four chapters (2, 3, 6, and 7) are being published for the first time. Many scholars have also read the chapters and have given helpful feedback.

The first chapter of the book, "Ethical Methodology: Between Public Theology and Public Policy" which was published in the *Journal of Religion and Business Ethics* in January 2010 has been downloaded over 1939 times in 36 months. This means that there are many teachers and students all over the world who are reading and using this paper in their classrooms. There is an appetite for an accessible and practical book on methodology and varieties of ethical analysis. Generally, all the published and unpublished essays have been well received by scholars and my students and I think this is a good time to make them available to a larger audience.

CHAPTER ONE

Ethical Methodology: Between Public Theology and Public Policy

Chapter Introduction

THAT PUBLIC THEOLOGY IS relevant to public policy debates and formulation should be self-evident. After all, public theologians aspire to develop ethical frameworks and discourses about how we should live together in plural civil societies. Public theology is offered as a form of discourse.[1] Unfortunately, contemporary public theologians have largely failed to develop models for ethical analysis directly appropriate for public discourse and relevant to public policy decision-making. While they have developed methods and theologies for understanding and interpreting the nature and dynamics of civil society, including the emerging global civil society, they have not explicitly provided a procedural method of ethical analysis that is informed by public theology.

In this chapter, I propose an ethical methodology as a form of public discourse, a model that incorporates the insights of public theology. Public theology has rejected theology as a discourse that withdraws into a spiritual gated community of sectarian isolation. It has equally rejected ways of speaking about the reality of God and God's will that are not valid in the

---

1. As Max Stackhouse puts it:
   [P]ublic theology intends to selectively put modernizing developments on a more secure basis by exposing, and where appropriate correcting, the submerged theological assumptions that are internal to them and sustaining them. Such an intent entails the belief that theology as a critical and constructive discipline is, properly, a *mode of public discourse* that both interprets the key areas of the common life in ways indispensable to the historical and social sciences, by pointing out the religious and ethical presuppositions that are operating in a given ethos, and simultaneously offers normative ethical guidance for the reformation and sustenance of a viable civil society, the basis of civilization. (*Globalization and Grace*, 85; italics added. See also 91–99, 112.)

contested common that is the modern civil society. It has instead proposed an understanding of ethics that speaks socially and theologically to the developments and issues of our times, and has taken the position that theology is capable of investigating —"according to the highest standards of truth and justice that are known and debated in reasonable discourse"—the relative validity of various religious claims about how civil society should operate.[2] It has also taken on the responsibility of clarifying the religious and ethological foundations of policies and ideas that shape civil society.

In the model of ethical analysis that I am proposing I show how public theologians can come into an informed judgment on public policies in the light of how people ought to live in civil society. It provides a robust "mechanics," which is ideationally rooted in public theology and deliberately crafted, to aid both experienced theologians and students to prepare ethical analyses for public discourse in a pluralistic society like the United States.

As a teacher in one of America's oldest seminaries I have to parse together from various works a discernible pattern or method of analysis to train my students in public theological-ethical analyses. When teaching public theology, I am interested in not only leading students through the history, themes, and debates in the field, but also in training them to be good ethical analysts in the public sphere. I have encountered students who wanted to work for public policy institutes where they thought they might be in positions to influence public policy debates from informed theological standpoints. Similarly, there have been students who wanted to serve the traditional parish pulpits but also desired to acquire the competence to analyze public policies from a public theology perspective. There has not been a handy and readily available model to guide such beginners in the practice. With this chapter I hope to fill the gap, to creatively advance the development of public theology.

My desire to fill the gap is not just about giving (would-be) ethicists another instrument in their toolbox. But to convey to them the notion that ethics is a methodical form of reason and speech. This is fundamental to understanding public theology as a form of public discourse and discerning from what philosophical position it sallies forth into the public arena. It is important to note right away that ethics as reason and speech is not about the process of an ethicist *reasoning* through a problem and voicing his or her thought about the moral fabric of society. What I have in mind is much more fundamental. I am here thinking of ethics as a process that unlocks

---

2. Stackhouse, "Introduction," 10–34.

the power of truth, justice, and harmony embodied in any form of human sociality. This process of unlocking truth, justice, and harmony is not aimed at providing the means or wisdom for perfecting the bureaucratic management of any current social order or sociality—although this is an aspect of reason we will call technical reason. But there is also ontological reason, which is really about the determination of the proper ends, *teleoi*, of any form of human sociality.[3] Ethics points us to ends beyond the existing forms of human sociality. It insists that an existing order can find those ends beyond itself only when its agents rise beyond themselves.

Reason is principally about the determination of ends of human sociality. These are ends that should point us beyond the existing forms of human sociality, to move our gaze further beyond ourselves. Reason is the source of meaning; it is the search for fulfillment; it represents an inescapable moral call on humanity to deepen and widen being. Ontological reason is the precondition for technical reason. Ontological reason is the process in which technical reason reaches beyond itself and its world. Ontological reason is the movement of technical reason toward ultimate meaning and significance. Technical reason is the presupposition of ontological reason, and ontological reason is the fulfillment of technical reason. The two concepts of reason are in means-end relationship. Technical reason deals with the discovery of the means of actualization of human potentials. Ontological reason is the longing for the source of all meaning, the driving force toward the good itself.[4]

In this quest for fulfillment our brains, voices, and bodies are all involved in both resisting existing orders that absolutize themselves and in forging and straining toward a new window of "else-where" and "else-when." This idea of window points us toward both what is present and what is absent in an extant order. In ethics we are trying to paint a portrait of our community and/or the subject of our focus. The portrait becomes a space (a "rectangle" for example) through which the community or the subject is seen. But it also provides the lens, perspective to see what is absent in the community. Like all windows, an "ethical-window" marks the boundary between what is currently obtained (what is inside the house) and what is

---

3. Practical reasoning (wisdom) as the ability to exercise sound judgment and discerning of the best means to attain goals is part of the deliberative process that goes into technical reasoning which is about finding the means (wisdom) and technical mastery for attaining and advancing an end or goal. Ontological reasoning is about the determination of proper ends and the ultimate vision that should guide society.

4. Tillich, *Systematic Theology*, 1:72–77.

outside, what we can strive for in the open, unconfined space. Through this window we are trying to see what is outside of ourselves, outside of our current existing order, but it is not always totally transparent; we see through an inherited (though continually reworked) mental representation. We are trying to see the world, the cosmos outside, through our particular *throwness* into the world.

Theological-ethical reasoning is in large part an attempt to provide a window on creativity and an avenue to show how the creative principles at work in human coexistence and the larger cosmos can be harnessed for human flourishing (*eudaimonia* in the Aristotelian sense). It is an ordered speech that attempts to link forms of human sociality to perceived[5] inner thrust of God's liberatory activity in the world. In other words, ethics attempts to relate the inner life of social institutions to the invisible rhythms and creative force that sustain and move the universe. (I have here in mind Paul Tillich's notion of theonomous ethics.)

Mechanics of Ethical Methodology

Let me now state how the second part of this chapter will unfold. There are three sections in the second part: the first section lays out a philosophy of ethical analysis. It develops some insights about ethical analysis that serve as gangway connecting the notion of ethics in the above introductory remarks and the practical, nitty-gritty task of constructing a meta-ethical model. Based on the philosophy developed, I describe in the second section the appropriate methodology for doing theological-ethical analyses of social problems. It is important to mention that the methodical steps spread out in this section are not like a cookbook recipe. In preparing food, attention to the recipe has an end other than itself, but the methodology adumbrated here does not; good and effective methodology in itself is an end. Cooking is an activity of producing something beyond the cooking act itself. In contrast, ethical methodology as understood by this author is the

---

5. I carefully chose the word, perceived, to indicate that human perception of God's activities in the world is always a particular decision. "We *must* make decisions about where God is at work so we can join in the fight against evil. But there is no perfect guide for discerning God's movement in the world. Contrary to what many conservatives would say, the Bible is not a blueprint on this matter. It is a valuable symbol for pointing to God's revelation in Jesus, but it is not self-interpreting. We are thus placed in an existential situation of freedom in which the burden is on us to make decisions without a guaranteed ethical guide." Cone, *Black Theology of Liberation*, 7; italics in the original.

activity of doing ethics well as such. Methodology is not fundamentally the production of "goods external" to the ethical reasoning, but the excellence or perfection of "internal goods," goods constituting the internal aims of the social practice of public theology. I conclude with final remarks in the last section. Specifically, I uncover the deep theological-social theoretic assumptions that are internal to the model.

A Philosophy of Ethical Analysis

The first thing the student needs to know in the task of analysis is the answer to this important question: "what is ethical analysis?" Ethical analysis is about identifying a problem that threatens the moral fabric and stability of society, showing how the particular problem has moved it away from that which underlies its existence and expresses itself in it as the ultimate concern, and indicating that by solving the problem the society will be brought in close responsiveness to its ultimate concern. This rather lengthy definition has three components:

a. Analysis of the problem;
b. Relating the problem to the ultimate concern, ultimate reality, of the community, and
c. Offering suggestions for solution that will strengthen the moral fabric of the community and move it closer to the principles of its ultimate concern.

Every society or tradition has certain categories, concepts, and images from which to draw and root the analysis when executing "b" and "c" above. It makes eminent sense to examine—even if only preliminarily—moral problems through them. The purpose is to show how the various dimensions of the problem and the community that bears its burden are illuminated when understood in relation to the moral and spiritual constructs of the community. One such category, concept or construct is the ultimate reality or concern. The ultimate concern is the orientation for life, the ultimate point of reference. This is usually taken as God; but sometimes it is a philosophical absolute (like eudaimonia, rational order, will-to-power). It is about that which is most important, which is taken seriously as the deepest and most fundamental.

The importance given to the ultimate concern in the solution determines whether the analysis is regarded as a theological-ethical one or social-ethical one. It is theological-ethical if the author takes as her ultimate

Methods of Ethical Analysis

point of reference God or a doctrine of God (*theos*). The construct of God (in dialectical inter-relationship with other theological terms) is used to grasp and interpret the crucial dimensions of the problem and its possible solution. It is social-ethical analysis if the doctrine of God is replaced by a philosophical construct or absolute.[6]

In the light of our elaboration of "b" and "c," above, let us recast the description of the task of ethical analysis. Ethical analysis is both a critical and constructive investigation of a social problem in the light of a community's ultimate point of reference for all life and its immediate environment. Unlike when the ethicist is writing ethical theories or laying out a philosophical treatise on ethics, which she hopes will one day serve as a point of reference for human behavior and investigation of social problems, public ethical analysis is about identifying obstacles to the realization of the promises in a society's construct of God or absolute and showing how to remove or overcome them in the name of that God or absolute. In faith (in terms of believing and showing concern about that which is considered absolute, ultimate), the ethical analyst works to remove all obstacles to the vision of the good life or the common good. She is constantly and deliberately searching for obstacles to be overcome in the hope of realizing the good life, eudaimonia, the kingdom of God, or the common good. Does she ever reach the end of this process? Nein! This is so because, as Paul Tillich once put it, faith is concern about the ultimate. We never grasp this reality; it is always beyond our reach. So we are never rest content with the quality of humanization and humanness in a given human sociality. Faith in God (the ultimate reality, point of reference) invites us to test all our human creations to see and judge whether there is something greater or better in the horizon and to always press on to it.

In a certain sense, ethical analysis is faith seeking resistance. This seeking aims to overcome resistance to the common good in the name of the ultimate principle. So every genuine ethical analysis aims at the overcoming of resistance. The ethicist is driven to her task by an urge to overcome that

---

6. Some readers may find the distinction between theological-ethical and social-ethical analysis questionable because the difference between them is only attributed to whether an ethical analysis refers to God (gods) or a philosophical construct as the ultimate concern of society. The distinction is further muddled by the fact that there are philosophical constructs of God. I have made this crude distinction only to gesture to the idea that in a pluralistic society there are some who may believe in God (whether that deity is personal, anthropomorphic, biblical or not) and others who do not believe in God or are agnostic and thus prefer to erect a non-God, non-divine philosophical ideal as the ultimate point of reference for orientation to life. It is only in this sense that I want the distinction to be interpreted.

Ethical Methodology: Between Public Theology and Public Policy

does not necessarily aim to dominate and control. She thirsts to confront and overcome the ideas, problems, groups, institutions, and any form of resistance that threatens the moral fabric of the society and in so doing oppose the satisfaction of the society's ultimate principle. The urge never rests because the principle can never be realized concretely. Her deliberate quest for resistance cannot be satisfied. The ethicist never comes to the point or state of affairs in which all resistance has been overcome because the ideal in the name of which she struggles is always in the future. An ethicist's work is never done. Hers is an activity in pursuit of an else-where and else-when land of "pure delight," the ultimate human good. The ethicist struggles against all that stands in the way of the common good. In other words, she strives until the paramount goal or end of her community is attained—nay, it can only be asymptotically approached. In reality, she never adjudges her society as having reached that level of human flourishing where all strivings for truth, justice, and harmony have stopped.

In conclusion, let me state that every genuine ethical analysis in any society is set in motion by four conditions. First, there is an ultimate concern that serves as a telos of society. Ethics is a search for God and how God is revealed in humanity and in the struggles for human flourishing. Basically, to undertake theological ethics is to search for God in the midst of history and to relate a community's understanding of the nature of ultimate reality and its derived truth to the logic and dynamics of human sociality. The truth we are talking about here is an anthropocentric, earthly, one. It is a truth, though sourced from an understanding of the ultimate; is pre-formed, formed, and in-formed and is appropriated through an encounter with a concrete humanity, the reality of a people at a specific historical juncture.

This power of truth touches ground, as my former teacher, Professor Peter Paris would say, when it is on the side of human freedom and affirms human flourishing in its broadest meaning. Thus the search for God is, in a certain sense, a search for human freedom and flourishing in the name of an "ought to be." In terms of the prophetic tradition of the Israelite prophets of the Bible, the "ought to be" is a demand for justice in the name of Yahweh, in the name of the principle that implies ultimacy and universality. The God in whose name the "ought to be" is given and sustained is "the God of justice, who because he represents justice for everybody and every nation, is called the universal God, the God of the universe."[7] The "ought to be" stands as a critique of the present situation and drives it beyond to an

---

7. Tillich, *Dynamics of Faith*, 3.

utopological-progressive state of communion between human beings and between God and humans.

Now let us focus on the rest of the conditions that set ethical analysis in motion. The second condition is this: there are (perceived) obstacles and resistance to the realization of the "ought to be." Third, there is a desire to overcome such resistance by the power of one's analysis that can induce political will and social action to alter the prevailing situation. An ethical analysis is not completely a dispassionate exercise. It involves a vision or desire to change certain social circumstances, the *eros* to aid a given society to reach a higher level of human flourishing. Finally, the ethical analyst must be willing to oppose her proffered solutions because no solution or institution is timeless. They must all be subjected to the demands of the incoming future. Every generation must be allowed to be creative in its own terms. Every age must seek for its "permanent" laws and institutions which must be washed away like sand castles at the beach, if need be, by the crashing waves of the incoming future. Ethical analysis is an activity of creative destruction. The ethicist who is unwilling to surpass that which she has created or inherited in the name of that which encompasses and transcends her "heirloom" has not fully grasped the notion of ethics as the science of harnessing the creative principles at work in existential conditions for human flourishing or the common good.

The Methodology of Ethical Analysis

> An inquiry in social ethics should begin with some actual, concrete problems arising among human beings in their public actions. That is to say, such an investigation should begin with some conflicting views about the good that humans can and should do. . . . The result of such an investigation should be some resolution of the problem or a restatement of the problem in order to liberate the agents and their activities and to establish thereby the conditions for more creative enterprise.[8]

It is now time to sketch the network of analyses that constitutes ethical analysis and give determinate content to the philosophical position I have just sketched out.[9] For the sake of convenience, I will divide the process

---

8. Paris, *Black Religious Leaders*, 31–32.

9. I would like to thank Professors Max Stackhouse and Mark Taylor of Princeton Theological Seminary for their comments on an earlier version of this section in 2007.

Ethical Methodology: Between Public Theology and Public Policy

of ethical analysis into three major segments or stages: (1) Social or ethos analysis, (2) Resources for reflecting on the problem, and (3) Ethical solution and payoff. At the end of the presentation of the three segments, I will provide a flowchart that summarizes the contents of the stages and how they are articulated.

It is germane to mention at this juncture that the task of ethical analysis is not only about public issues and pursuit of social justice. Ethics definitely includes personal conduct, individual fairness, and our actions and behaviors in the private spheres. In this chapter, for our limited purpose as informed by the nature of public theology, the ethical is limited to the social, the common, spheres of human coexistence.

Ethics is also concerned with corporate behaviors that are in the public sphere. This chapter has not explicitly addressed business ethics. Nonetheless, it contains insights and ideas for business ethics. The focus of the chapter is on ethical methodology for public policy (or public policy debates), which covers economic ethics and the economy. Economic ethics and economy encompass business (corporate) ethics and businesses.

If a public policy is going to be enacted to cover businesses—an important segment of the public—then the methodology as explained applies to such a process. And if a corporation is thinking of jumping into a public debate in a pluralistic society likes ours it can follow the methodology of the chapter to craft its argument. It may not use God as the ultimate concern, but can formulate another supreme good. The chapter makes provision for alternative views of ultimate concern, supreme good, or philosophical construct. The methodology of this chapter will not be of much use to the analyst who thinks of business ethics in the narrow sense of "legal ethics," that is, the covering of bases to avoid liabilities and injury to public reputation of corporations, and staying out of obvious legal troubles.

Social Analysis

Every ethical analysis starts with a definition of the problem or a description of the ethical concern. This is the issue(s) that the ethicist considers to be threatening the moral fabric and stability of the society or community. The analyst needs to state clearly and precisely why the issue identified is a social problem and why the citizens need to focus on eliminating or ameliorating it.

Once the problem is adequately identified or laid out, the analyst undertakes a social-scientific examination of it; examines the "signs of the

Methods of Ethical Analysis

times" so to speak. She draws from social sciences, humanities, sciences, and other disciplines to help her audience understand the problem in its crucial dimensions. It pays or helps to provide some empirical analyses backed by historical and contemporary data. In this portion of the analysis she aims to take into consideration the multiple forces or propensities that structure a society and its problems.

What comes next is an examination of the ethos (the web of values, norms, organizing principles, etc.) of the society and how it relates to the problem. Here again the ethicist relies on the work of specialists to discern the ethos. Why is ethos analysis important? If the ethicist wants to change anything, she has got to understand the presuppositions behind it; wrestle with values that are implicit in the culture, comprehend values that drive the legitimacy (rightness or goodness) of actions and behaviors. There are resources in every community to draw from in analyzing an ethical problem. There are traditions, constitutions, laws, and exemplars of moral excellence to bring forth to bear on the problem and its possible solution. This brings us to the next segment of the methodological process of ethical analysis.

Resources for Reflecting on the Problem

At this phase or dimension of the analysis, the ethicist discusses the theological, biblical (sacred texts), or philosophical resources that she will bring to inform and shape the discourse of the problem. This is done with an eye to grounding and funding possible ethical solution, paradigm, or response to the problem. The overall aim of this sub-segment is for the ethicist to state her theology (theological, philosophical, presuppositions) for funding solutions. Every search for solution to an ethical problem presupposes a theological or philosophical understanding of humans and their place in the world in relation to their God or ultimate principle.

The analyst may not always have a pre-existing theology to bring to bear on the problem. Thus, she may need to develop a fresh theology in the light of the issues before her. The important thing to note here is the need to articulate the vision or concept of an ultimate reality that both undergirds the community and can legitimize the solution to the problem. The vision is either appropriated from an existing fund or is constructed (reconstructed) afresh.

The reflection on a problem for the purpose of crafting a relevant solution to an ethical problem should not be limited to theological deliberations alone. It is to involve and requires a rigorous analysis of the operating norms in the ethos (dis-covered by ethology) to see if they are appropriate. Appropriateness may be evaluated from two angles: right and good; that is, deontologically and teleologically.[10] In deontological terms, the analyst would like to know if the operating norms are in accord with the best knowledge available theologically by common grace. That is, to see whether they are in accord with the "laws of God." Teleologically, the question is: Are they in accord with the best theological vision of the purposes of God we can know? Of course, the analyst not working with the symbol of God can still do the deontological and teleological investigations by using other constructs such as Kant's categorical imperative or Aristotle's eudaimonia (flourishing life, happiness). In all of this, the analyst is inquiring as to what resources in the ethos can contribute to a solution or better solution. More importantly, the analyst wants to find out "whether what is going on ought to go on . . . Are the functioning principles and governing goals valid?"[11] On this note, the second major segment of the methodological flowchart (see *Stage 2* below) comes to a close and we shall now proceed to the next and final segment.

Ethical Solution (Responses, Paradigm) and Payoff

There are six doorways to traverse at this phase of the analysis that is largely prescriptive. They offer, as Max Stackhouse puts it, "guidance about how we might, insofar as it is possible, form a more valid ethos and develop those attitudes, institutions, habits, policies, and programs that are in accord with a more ethically viable ethos, rightly legitimated by a valid theological view of ultimate reality."[12]

At this point, the analyst has clearly identified the social problem, its impact on the moral fabric of the given community, and has pointed her audience to the theological and philosophical resources she hopes can offer valuable insights in the search for solution. Now she is ready to suggest solution. This is the first of the six doorways she has to traverse. The background question that drives her discourse at this stage is: What is the ethical solution (response, idea, paradigm, or intuition) that flows from my theological analysis (discourse) that bears upon the problem? Her task here must remain incomplete until she shows how her vaunted solution either strengthens the community or ameliorates (resolves, restates) the identified problem.

10. Stackhouse, "General Introduction," in Stackhouse and Paris, *God and Globalization*, 1:12–14.
11. Ibid., 1:11.
12. Ibid., 1:16.

Second, the presentation of the "solution" should be informed by a dialogue with important thinkers in the field. Ethicists are not gods who pronounce solutions from Olympian heights. Thus an ethicist is expected to show how her preferred solution is better than those offered by other scholars or how it improves on existing practices of the community.

Third, once the solution is well defined and defended, the ethicist must show how it fits into the ethos of the community discussed in "Resources for Reflection on the Problem" above. The analyst tells her audience why her solution should be considered a fitting response by the community at the given historical juncture in which it finds itself. Asking how the proposed solution fits or does not easily fit into the ethos may require confrontation or transformation of the ethos in that respect.

Next the analyst needs to ask herself, "do I need to propose new institution or organization to effect the necessary changes or support the realization of the proposed solution? If her answer is yes, she must determine the cost-benefit impact of establishing the new institution in the community. She goes to this length because she needs to convince decision-makers that her solutions will benefit society.

Fifth, many societies in the world are now pluralistic, and thus a public ethical analysis needs to adapt to this reality if it is to be taken seriously. In the postmodern world that we live in today—with its characteristic lack of a common sacred canopy over the public square—demands that an analyst must make a case for her values and solutions to perceived problems in the public domain. The ethical analysis is incomplete until the author addresses herself to these pertinent questions: How will my solution be perceived in a pluralistic civil society with multiple religions and worldviews? Will it pass muster with some academic viewpoints employed in the social-scientific examination of "Resources for Reflection on the Problem" above? What are some of the deontological, ethological, and teleological aspects of my proposed solutions (response) that can serve to build or uphold common morality (common good) in an open civil society?

Finally, what are the possible payoffs to the community if the proposed solution or response is accepted and adopted? In working out the payoffs, it is important for the analyst to bear in mind that benefits and costs are not always expressible in calculatable short-run economic terms. She may need to find other ways of illustrating the costs and benefits.

I have presented the steps for ethical analysis, but ethics is not only about analysis. It is also about social action. So it is important to situate our methodology within the context of social action informed by social or ethical principles. The ethical methodology we have just developed enables the ethicist or activist to do two things. First, to clearly see, understand, and judge (based on one's theological or philosophical principles) the state of the problem; second, to identify the most fitting solutions which can address the problem in the light of one's theology or social principles, and pluralism. These should lead to the final stage of action, praxis. The real purpose of analysis is to recognize the ways in which to act in order to change the circumstances that threaten the common good. Pope John XXIII put it well in his May 15, 1961 encyclical letter, *Mater et Magistra*, when he stated:

> There are three stages which should normally be followed in the reduction of social principles into practice. First, one reviews the concrete situation; secondly, one forms a judgment on it in the light of these same principles; thirdly, one decides what in the circumstances can and should be done to implement these principles. These are the three stages that are usually expressed in the three terms: look, judge, act.[13]

Flowchart of Ethical Analysis

In the preceding pages I set out the "mechanics" of executing an ethical analysis. I also briefly located the analysis in the context of an overarching purpose of social action. It bears noting that the methodology that has been presented is an ideal format. Most ethicists do not religiously follow this step-by-step approach. They often use a network approach—looping in and out of these stages in a non-sequential manner. The important thing is that the various elements, segments, or stages we have laboriously laid out are discernible in their works. A good and rigorous ethical analysis will always define or state the problem it intends to address, give a sense of the theological (philosophical or ethological) resources it is using to shape the discourse, and fund the offering of solution to the problem. Of course, not

13. Pope John XXIII, *Mater et Magistra*. It is tempting to at this point to consider the major social encyclicals that tackle issues of social justice and public theology that are in indicated in this chapter. To do this will take us too far afield as this chapter is only concerned with developing an ethical methodology for public theology, not with the concrete and specific analysis of any social issue. It will also be interesting to see how the ethical methodology of the major social encyclicals fits or does not fit with the method developed in this chapter. This is yet another task that we must let pass for now.

every analyst will endeavor to present each of these three dimensions in the manifold richness of a unified and coherent discourse as I have endeavored to present in this chapter. I have explicitly presented an ideal format implicit in the majority of good ethical analyses.[14] The purpose is to enable students to clearly follow the pedagogy of ethical analysis. Below is the summary of the methodology in a "flowchart" format for quick reference.

Stage 1: Social Analysis (Ethos Analysis)

a. What is the problem or concern? Why is it a problem? This is the issue(s) that you consider to be threatening the moral fabric and stability of the society or community.

b. Social-scientific examination of the problem. Draw from social sciences, humanities, sciences, etc. to help others understand the problem in its crucial dimensions. It pays or helps to provide some empirical analyses backed by historical and contemporary data. *This is one way of taking into account the multiple forces that structure a society.*

c. Examination of the ethos (values, norms, etc.) of the society and how it relates to the problem. *If you want to change anything you have got to understand the presuppositions behind it. Wrestle with the values that are implicit in the culture, values that drive the legitimacy (rightness or goodness) of actions/behaviors.*

Stage 2: Resources for Reflecting on the Problem

a. Identify theological and biblical (philosophical) resources that will be brought to inform and shape the discourse of the problem and also ground and fund possible ethical solution, paradigm, response. *What is your theology (or theological presuppositions) for approaching the problem?*

b. Analyze the operating norms in the ethos (discovered by ethology) to see if they are basically right (deontologically, that is, in accord with the best knowledge available theologically by

---

14. For examples of the use of this methodology in ethical analysis see Wariboko, *Depth and Destiny of Work*; Wariboko, *God and Money*; Taylor, *Executed Gods*; Volf, *Exclusion and Embrace*; Yong, *Theology and Down Syndrome*.

common grace or in accord with the "laws of God"). And see if they are also actually good (teleologically, that is, in accord with the best theological vision of the purposes of God we can know).

Stage 3: Ethical Solution (Response, Paradigm) and Payoff

    a. What is the ethical solution (response, idea, paradigm, intuition) that flows from your theological analysis/discourse that bears upon the problem? Show how it can either strengthen the community or reduce (remove, restate, solve) the identified problem.

    b. This "solution" should be framed by dialogue with important thinkers in the field.

    c. Once the solution is well defined, show how it fits into the ethos of the community identified in *Stage* 1 above. Explain why your solution should be considered a fitting response by the community that is at a given historical juncture. Asking how the proposed solution fits or does not easily fit into the ethos may require confrontation or transformation of the ethos in that respect. Inquire also as to what resources in the ethos could contribute to a better solution.

    d. Determine whether a new institution or organization needs to be proposed in order to effect the necessary changes. If so, what is the cost-benefit impact of this new institution on the community?

    e. Discern how your solution will be perceived in a pluralistic civil society with multiple religions and worldviews. Will it also pass muster with some of the academic viewpoints you identified and used in *Stage* 1 (social-scientific examination). *What are some of the deontological, ethological, and teleological aspects of your proposed response/solution that can serve to build or uphold common morality (common good) in an open civil society?*

    f. What are the possible overall payoffs to the community if your solution or response is accepted and adopted? *Remember, benefits are not always expressible in calculatable short-run economic terms.*

Methods of Ethical Analysis

Concluding Remarks

By way of reaching conclusion, I would like to briefly lay out the *deep structure* beneath the ethical model of analysis presented above. What I have submitted as a model is a discourse that attempts to relate ultimate ends, theological presuppositions, to social reality, social sciences, ethos, and pluralism. It is rooted in a Troeltschian discourse of how to relate the formal spirit of the church to the material realities that constitute the civil society, to the goods and purposes of the inner-worldly life. One of Ernst Troeltsch's contributions to Christian ethics is to show how the church was able to bring together in unity the transcendent goals of Christianity and cultural values as it engages its public. The ethical methodology of this chapter has shown how the theologian can navigate the problematic relation between Christianity and culture, can mediate the tension between (religious) Christian moral purposes and humane ethical motivation without retreating behind sectarian walls. As Brent W. Sockness argues:

> The modern religious crisis is an ethical and cultural one not to be solved by writing new dogmatic treatises. The question is how to mediate and hold together the tense polarity between religious and humane morality, or, to borrow Troeltsch's illustration, how to square the piety of Luther and Bach, on the one hand, with the humanity of Goethe and the statesmanship of Bismarck, on the other hand.... For Troeltsch, the exploration of the "fundamental problems of ethics" is largely a matter of developing a conceptual scheme or set of categories capable of doing justice to the nature of moral reality as we find it historically and actually experience it.[15]

The model has shown us a simple way to make Christian (religious) ideas relevant to social issues even when they infinitely transcend the social and ultimately pull it toward God's purposes. Put differently, it reveals how theological ethics or public theology can move away from conceptual analyses to engage with concrete policy discourse on social problems. This engagement with policies and with contemporary history is necessary to make public theology practical. The rigors of a deliberate and well thought-out ethical analysis can offer practical guidance to decision-makers as they deal with the urgent issues of our time.

There is another aspect of the deep structure of the model worth pointing out in order to further expose the submerged theological-social

---

15. Sockness, "Looking Behind the Social Teachings," 243–44.

theoretical assumptions that are internal to it and also sustain it. The ethical analysis I have developed in this chapter does not only attempt to grasp the social analysis and empirical reality of problems, but also strives to plumb the depths of the presuppositions about human nature and community's understanding of God in its discourse. The thinking is that without the analyst understanding the deep presuppositions, the deepest and broadest ethos of forms of human sociality she might miss the vital non-material motivating factors for/against a public policy, ethical reforms within the economy and society, or the pursuit of the common good. As Stackhouse, one of America's eminent ethicists, has argued, public theologians enter into debates about political and economic policies based on the conviction that the political economy—and indeed all civilizations—are deeply influenced by religion, worldview, and ethical presuppositions.[16] Stackhouse is, of course, drawing from what Max Weber taught us long ago. Weber argued that religion is an independent factor that substantively shapes culture and economic systems in particular are influenced by religious factors that are in constant interaction with material interests.[17]

Having said all this, I would like to state that neither public theology nor the ethical methodology described in this chapter is about giving direction to governmental policy. Both of them—at least as I understand them—are aimed at recognizing the religious dynamics that influence social life. Whether we are talking about public theology in its thematic-discursive format or in its analytical-methodological format as presented in this chapter the attention is on the need to develop capabilities that address and guide the basic ordering of the common life in non-particularistic theological terms. The overarching intention is to present arguments that promote greater inclusiveness, greater justice, and higher levels of human flourishing that spur on men and women to transformative praxis.

---

16. Stackhouse, *Globalization and Grace*, 4:77–116.
17. Weber, *Economy and Society*. See also his *Protestant Ethic*.

Chapter Two

Jeffrey Stout's Theory of Public Reason

Opening Word

THIS CHAPTER GOES INTO why we do what we do as ethicists or thinkers on ethical methodology. Why does a careful method of ethical analysis or reasoning matter in a pluralistic democratic society? What kind of reason a successful ethical methodology hopes to put forward in a public debate and what kind of society demands such reason?

The methodology we have proposed in the previous chapter assumes that the ethicist lives in a community in which citizens are committed to exchanging reasons and holding one another responsible for their actions. If we are not to resort to physical violence or the sheer bullying of majority vote, then giving and exchanging reasons for public actions and policies is the preferred method of settling differences of opinion. There is no gainsaying the importance of a properly crafted ethical methodology in the giving and exchanging of reasons and moral judgment in democratic public domain.

The methodology of ethics we have laid out in chapter 1 is about the mechanics of carefully formulating public reasons for public policies so others could reasonably accept them as a basis for public actions. What makes a reason public instead of being private? In this chapter, we attempt to answer this question with a close reading of Jeffrey Stout's *Democracy and Tradition* against the background of David Hume's moral theory of "general point of view."

Chapter Introduction[1]

> The more we converse with mankind, and the greater social intercourse we maintain, the more shall we be familiarized to these general preferences and distinctions, without which our conversation and discourse could scarcely be rendered intelligible to each other. It is necessary for us, in our calm judgments and discourse concerning the characters of men, to neglect all these differences, and render our sentiments more public and social. The intercourse of sentiments, therefore, in society and conversation, makes us form some general unalterable standard, by which we may approve of characters and manners. (Hume, *Enquiries*, 5: 228, 229.)

> All democratic citizens should feel free, in my view, to express whatever premises actually serve as reasons for their claims. The reasons that are [acceptable] not just any reason. When proposing a political policy one should do one's best to supply reasons for it that people occupying other points of view could reasonably accept. No ethical community could sustain a discursive practice without imposing on each of its members the necessity of keeping track of the normative attitudes and entitlements of their interlocutors, because without this there would be no communication—and therefore no exchange of reasons—among them. (Stout, *Democracy and Tradition*, 10, 65, 280.)

The architecture of Hume's moral theory, which is based on the "general point of view"[2] on sentiments, arguably forms the template (flowchart) of the arguments concerning public reason that Jeffrey Stout used in his *Democracy and Tradition*. Both authors argue that moral distinctions may begin with incorrect sentiments or private reasons and are corrected by the adoption of the general point of view or the citizen's point of view. This chapter examines and uncovers the shared "architectonics," structural design of their theories. I have discovered that not only are their themes related but the ways in which the sub themes and arguments are related to one another are also quite similar. That is to say Hume's and Stout's arguments are not just structurally similar, but also similar at the level of detail. The unveiling of the ordered structure beneath the flow of philosophical

---

1. I wish to thank Professor Michael Smith, Philosophy Department, Princeton University, Princeton, New Jersey, for his comments on an earlier version of this paper.

2. For an excellent introduction to the general point of view see Davie, "Hume's General Point of View," 275–94.

language and arguments that are centuries apart shows that both Hume and Stout have produced brilliant theories through the expression of the same structure.

This writer does not pretend to investigate the systematic leanings of Hume and Stout; neither to offer any explicit or implicit notion of logical and formal systems in their thoughts nor to provide a discourse on their philosophical architectonics. What I am doing with Stout's *Democracy and Tradition* is akin to showing how Karl Marx's *Das Capital*, especially his understanding of money and capital, depends on Hegel's *Science of Logic*. Put differently, one can compare the similarity between Hume's moral theory and Stout's theory of public reason to that between West African Pidgin English and its indigenous languages. Pidgin English is principally and primarily the pouring of English words into the vessel of African syntax. It appears Stout has poured his fresh ideas and words into an old Humean "syntax." Stout unconsciously appropriates a Humean flowchart of argumentative moves, the structural design in the moral theory to develop his account of public reason. It is as if before Stout started writing he was privy to a Humean template that directed the flow, meanderings, and windings, and the rhapsodic state of his intuitions. It is this shared template that I hope to lay bare in this essay.

For both Stout and Hume the path to public morality (reason) is visualized as a big social orchestra where each player (citizen) tunes her "sentimental" ("religious") instrument to interact with other instruments to produce a symphony, but she is not allowed to play a solo tune to which all must dance. Given that he has allowed everyone to enter the public discursive exchange with their religious sentiments, Stout is concerned with how contradictions in such exchange of reasons can be transformed into a useable form of a pluralistic *conversation* that is protected from human tendencies to bias. According to him, public (moral) reason is not created by an independent moral tradition but arises out of concrete democratic public discourse. Similarly, Hume in his moral theory is concerned with how contradictions in sentiments can be transformed into a useable form in public morality given that everyone making moral judgment starts from his or her individual sentiments. Hume too rejected a universal moral sense and takes moral judgments as products of consensus, sort of a coincidence of sympathies which arises from the fertile soil of social discursive exchanges. Both Hume and Stout argue for a "standard" that has "universal reach" without insisting on *a* universal point of view that is abstracted from the ethical life of a people.

I do not think that any commentator on *Democracy and Tradition* has done full justice to Stout's simple, elegant structure of argumentative strategies and its deep affinity with Hume's moral theory based on the "general point of view" on sentiments. There is very little in Stout's structure of argumentation or thought that was not used or anticipated in Hume. I need to state that I cannot absolutely prove my point of similarity between Hume's and Stout's architectures. I can only present some examples and considerations that should make the point believable.

This chapter is divided into five sections. I begin with a discussion of the central themes and flows of arguments, from subjectivity to subject matter in both the moral theory of Hume and the public reason theory of Stout. From this section we begin to see commonality of structure that gives shape to their theories. Section two tackles the technical issue of the architecture of their theories in the sense of presenting the skeletal frame or the "flowchart" of their theories. On purpose I avoid the rhetoric of thick descriptions so as to parsimoniously show the embedded architectural similarity. The third section examines the similarity of the ambivalences in both theories. Hume's moral theory oscillates between (or holds in tension) utilitarianism and contractarianism. Stout's theory of public reason verges at the edge of pragmatism and traditionalism. Is there anything in the nature of the tasks they both undertook or in the shared architecture of their arguments that might just account for the ambiguities? Section four treats the crucial difference between the two theories. Concluding remarks follow in the final section.

Section One: Central Themes of Hume and Stout

Both authors set out to develop a theory of morality, public intercourse as not only a solution to problems the public faces but also the standard for the solution the public needs to adopt for the problem it would otherwise face. Morality for them is "the natural, reasonable, and indispensable product of problem-solving beings."[3] The problem that threatens civility and unity in society is traced to variable sentiments by Hume and attributed to religious values or to the liberal elite that want to exclude religious reasons from political debate by Stout.[4] The sentiments or values create problems because in a society with diverse interests we are unable to converse and avoid per-

---

3. Sayre-McCord, "Hume and the Bauhaus Theory," 281.
4. Hume, *Treatise*, 582; Stout, *Democracy and Tradition*, 4–7, 64.

petual contradictions if we all act on the basis of our personal point of view. When religious citizens express their religious convictions while exchanging reasons for their respective political views, Stout states that

> secular liberals find the resulting cacophony deeply disturbing. Some of them have strongly urged people to restrain themselves from bringing their religious commitments with them into the political sphere. Many religious people have grown frustrated at the unwillingness of the liberal elite to hear them out on their own terms, and have recently had much to say against the hypocrisies and biases of secularism. Freedom of religion now strikes some prominent theologians as a secularist ruse designed to reduce religion to insignificance.[5]

Hume frames his version of the problem as: "[We] everyday often meet with persons, who are in a different situation from ourselves, and who cou'd never converse with us on any reasonable terms, were we to remain constantly in that situation and point of view which is peculiar to us."[6]

The solution to these continual and aching contradictions is the general point of view or the public reason criterion. "In order, therefore, to prevent these continual *contradictions*, and arrive at a more *stable* judgment of things, we fix on some *steady* and *general* points of view; and always, in our thoughts, place ourselves in them, whatever may be the present situation."[7] For Stout, democracy is a discursive practice that moves and has its being in the *social practice* of giving and asking for ethical reasons. These reasons are used by citizens in a democracy to call one another to account and on deciding on institutional arrangements and political policies. According to him, social practices are procedural and normative activities that are considered constitutive of a social system. They are normative because they harbor within them substantive commitments that guide and condition the procedures used to always call participants to account.[8]

I need to quickly state a caveat to this reading of Hume and Stout. One has not discerned that both authors are arguing that all solutions to moral problems were consciously designed or introduced even though they recognize morality as solutions to problems. In fact, Stout argues in chapters 8 and 11 that moral principles only make explicit norms that are

---

5. Stout, *Democracy and Tradition*, 64.
6. Hume, *Treatise*, 603.
7. Hume, *Treatise*, 581–82; italics in the original.
8. Stout, *Democracy and Tradition*, 4–5.

already implicit in the practical inferential commitments of a community that exchanges reasons and holds one another responsible for their actions.

Granted that caveat, we need to proceed and ask this question: If morality is a solution to problems and given that a society cannot solve all its problems, how does it decide on the morally relevant problems and the solutions that are suited to them? For Hume certain sets of problems become collectively salient given the frame and conditions of a society; and the relevant solutions among myriad ones are those that will alleviate the problems as much as possible.[9] This is also the approach followed by Stout who thinks that the rise of the Christian (cultural) Right and its effort to impose a particular Christian viewpoint on the rest of citizenry and the liberal left's denial of religious input in public discourse are the types of problems threatening the democratic fabric and future of America. The acceptable solution to this collectively salient problem is the principle of public reason (free public exchange of reasons).

The idea of morality as a solution to problems, as providing benefits to society, smacks of utilitarianism. Are moral solutions evaluated on the basis of usefulness, actual or expected utility? Both authors' theories of morality do not yield easily to such a characterization. Hume promotes the idea of "narrow circle" which denies usefulness as extending to overall consequences for everyone affected. He states that we "confine our view to that narrow circle, in which any person moves, in order to form a judgment of his moral character. When the natural tendency of his passions leads him to be serviceable and useful within this sphere, we approve of his character, and love his person, by a sympathy with the sentiments of those, who have more particular connexion with him."[10] In Stout's theory there are two notions of "narrow circle"—one explicit and the other implicit. The explicit one has to do with his notion of justification in reason-giving. He made a distinction between being able to justify a claim to one's actual *audience* and being able to justify it to all rational beings; and in this way rejects the need to ground political discussion in a set of rules no reasonable and rational citizen could reasonably reject.[11] His is a limited justification insofar as it relates to a circumscribed audience. His argument is worth quoting at length here:

---

9. Sayre-McCord, "Hume and the Bauhaus Theory," 286–87.
10. Hume, *Treatise*, 602.
11. Stout, *Democracy and Tradition*, 247, 296.

Methods of Ethical Analysis

Let us say that a justification of the claim P is an answer to the question, Why believe that P? If the answer is successful, we say that the claim in question is justified. In what, then, does success of a justification consist? In eliminating relevant reasons for doubting that P, what reasons for doubting P are relevant and what suffices for their elimination? That depends on context, in particular, on the people to whom the justification is addressed. Call the class of such people the justification's *audience*. Reasons for doubting P are relevant if they prevent or might prevent an epistemically competent and responsible member of the audience from being justified in believing that P. Relevant reasons for doubting P have been eliminated when everyone in the audience is justified in believing that P . . . . Justifications are answers to why-questions of a certain sort. As such, they are dependent on context: first, because conversational context determines the question to which a justification counts as an answer and thus the sort of information being requested; second, because conversational context determines a justification's audience; and third, because a justification's success can be appraised only in relation to its audience, including their relevant reasons for doubting and the commitments they are entitled to accept.[12]

Now let us shift focus to the implicit notion of "narrow circle" in *Democracy and Tradition*. Stout's concept of public reason or what he calls "democratic exchange of reasons" is not evaluated on the basis of consequences for everyone affected by it. In reality, Stout, while claiming to accommodate all viewpoints as initial premises for public debate, is actually advocating a theory of public reason in narrow circle, a paradoxically narrow circle. If the validity of his notion of public reason is to be assessed by the common democratic principle of one person one vote it will collapse as an arbitrary proposal. If public reason is not straitjacketed in narrow circle but widened and allowed to fly as a bird it will reflect the reasoning of the majority or be in deference to the majority and Stout stoutly rejects this. His whole interest in the notion of public reason is about how people who are not completely selfish, with diverse viewpoints and committed to living in a modern pluralistic democracy, might live well with themselves and others. Thus, he confines his concept of public reason to that narrow circle in which we can all coexist under the standard of "general survey." It is true that Stout, unlike John Rawls and Richard Rorty, wants us to come to the public square with our "clothes of values" on and not naked. It is truer

12. Ibid., 234–35.

to say he wants us to shed some of them before we enter the inner sanctum of the narrow circle of limited generosity, moderate clothing, and mutual dependence, where public deliberation and decisions are made. The appeal to public reason is not a utilitarian appeal to "benefits received by all who might be effected" but to the prospect of mutual advantage. Then, in terms of set theory, public reason adheres in the union of intersecting sets whose conjoined area is always narrower than that of the sum of the areas of the intersecting sets.

Both Hume's general point of view and Stout's theory of public reason are not appealing to benefits we will each derive for adopting either of them but to something that regulate our behavior and civil conduct in a society that strives to have a common mutually accessible standard for public morality. "When we form our judgments of persons, merely from the tendency of their characters to our own benefit, or to that of our friends," Hume suggests, "we find so many contradictions to our sentiments in society and conversation, and such an uncertainty from the incessant changes of our situations, that we seek some other standard of merit and demerit, which may not admit of so great variation."[13] Stout's quest to have his theory of public or democratic reason as the sought-after standard in public discursive practice and his call for Americans to come out of Hollinger's three formidable constituencies (jet-setting executives, Bible-thumping evangelicals, and ethnic-diasporic communities) is a cry for survival of democracy in America. "Democracy will face unpromising odds at the national level so long as the three entrenched constituencies jointly control the political landscape and behave as they are behaving."[14] The public reason theory—the free discursive practice of ethical deliberation and political debate and holding one another responsible for actions—corresponds to some kind of Humean standard. And it is pitched to earn wide allegiance and for identification with broader ethical inheritance and political community by "working to eliminate, or at least attenuate, the problems that come from each evaluating things from own point of view."[15] Stout wants Americans to fix on this concept of public reasoning and always in their thoughts and practices to place themselves in it, whatever may be their present situation.

---

13. Hume, *Treatise*, 319.

14. Stout, *Democracy and Tradition*, 292.

15. The portion of the sentence in quotation marks comes from Sayre-McCord, "Hume and the Bauhaus Theory," 291.

Hume and Stout, unlike ultra-restrictive liberals of today, want us to reach the general and disinterested "survey" by starting from our sentiments which both regard as inevitable in making judgments. They believe that citizens should not be divested of their sentiments and values in the public square or morality sphere but subject such to some common standard. In this regard, their moral theories are aimed at finding a common platform for conversation and judgment in the midst of citizens that are "clothed" with their sentiments. The general point of view or public reason is not meant to facilitate Christians, non-Christians, or any diverse group of persons to see things from the same perspective all the time or approve events and acts in the same way, but only to correct and calibrate peculiar, characteristic, and internal perceptions and judgment for the sake of public discourse. As Sayre-McCord puts it in assessing Hume's general and disinterested survey of moral taste, "this will not actually lead us to feel approval for everything towards which we would feel approval from that common point of view but it at least sets a standard and vocabulary with which we can converse about moral matters (while avoiding what would otherwise be an onslaught of contradictions and fluctuations)."[16]

The alternative to the shared standard for regulating evaluations or exchange of reasons is the draconian Hobbesian solution. But absolute ruler with absolute power will contradict the democratic traditions of America as Stout argues[17] or the notion of shared humanity as Hume argues,[18] which is the basis for the interaction. Even though people characters, dialectical locations, and statuses differ and they may differ in their responses to the general point of view or the theory of public reason, what grounds their intercourse or discursive practice and comes into play is either the common humanity or the piety to democratic tradition that they share.

There is just one more analysis of the broad themes or broad sweep of arguments to consider in Hume's and Stout's works before closing this premier section. In making the transition from sentiments, values, religious premises or viewpoints to public moral judgments or engagement, both philosophers made a two-stage movement. It is only by this technique that they were able to (or hope to) nudge people loaded down with peculiar sentiments and idiosyncratic points of view into the public square without a combustible, destructive, and noncommunicative interaction. They made

16. Ibid., 285.
17. Stout, *Democracy and Tradition*, 100, 126–27.
18. Hume, *Enquiries*, 273.

a subtle distinction between moral reaction (initial moral response or disposition) and moral judgment. Our individual sentiments, passions, and religious values will inevitably produce certain feelings, reactions, or indignations even when we are consciously subjecting our views to correction and moving towards a mutually accessible point of view. But moral judgments and pronouncements transcend this stage when they imbed corrections for distortions of perspective or for democratic commitments in the name of a general position—what Hume calls the "standard of moral taste."[19] Stouts calls it, among many other appellations, freedom constrained by norms, "conversation," expressive freedom.[20] According to Stout, the substance of a common democratic ethical life of a people does not reside in explicitly formulated abstract norms or peculiar reason of a group no matter how that groups tinkers its commitment to strive for expressive equilibrium. "It resides," Stout suggests, "in the myriad observations, material inferences, actions, and mutually recognitive reactions that constitute the dialectical process itself. This changes at least a bit with every discursive move that is made by every interlocutor."[21]

In the preceding paragraphs, I have argued that there are similarities in the broad sweep of arguments in both Hume's and Stout's moral theories. This set of similarities is rooted in two things:

a. Both authors allow all to come to the public square with their sentiments knowing full well that there will be contradictions.

b. An attempt to solve the contradictions arising from the free expression by defining a set of constraint by norms or standard located in the shared life or nature of a people.

In the next section, I investigate the tight structural design of their arguments.

There are also differences in their positions though both of them of think that the scope of justification is limited. There is a big difference between Hume's suggestion that we only take account of the effects of our actions on those in the narrow circle (the idea, in other words, that the effects of our actions on those outside the narrow circle do not matter morally) and Stout's idea that justification is always a matter of providing reasons for removing doubt to members of an audience (which is not the set of all reasonable and rational citizens). For the latter emphatically does not imply that those whose doubts we are not in the business of removing are

---

19. Ibid., 229; *Treatise*, 603.
20. Stout, *Democracy and Tradition*, 77–80, 112, 152–53, 175, 196–98.
21. Ibid., 79.

Methods of Ethical Analysis

not morally consider-able. Similarly, in the practical realm Stout's talk of a public discursive practice is not to be understood as a limitation on the scope of those of whom we have obligations.[22]

Section Two: Similarity in Architecture of Hume and Stout Moral Theories

Anyone trying to find similarities between concepts, cultures, and patterns of reasoning between any two groups or scholars enters the rough terrain of classification. She is either dismissed as seeing similarities where there are none, arbitrarily taking some aspects as relevant and others as not, or she is considered just not able to do such a daunting task rigorously. For instance, Nelson Goodman has argued that just any two objects, events, or modes of thought can have properties in common.[23] Sameness is not intrinsic to any object, Goodman argues, but is conferred and as such similarity as a basis of categorization does not explain much. I will argue that there is something substantive in my similarity thesis by showing how the constraints in the common structure of their arguments control how the parts of their theory interact.

This still may not satisfy the class of critics who generally set an impossibly high bar for the test of similarity. Such scholars argue that there are just too many concerns to deal with for such an exercise to be deemed successful. One has to find the acceptable means of making comparison: What ought to count as similarities in a given context and in what respects? What about surface or deeper similarities? What is the concern that determines the acceptable degree of similarity? Even when one is successful in demonstrating uniformities there is still the matter of showing what practical and explanatory purpose they will serve. On the matter of common morality, Stout himself writes that, "overall similarity is itself a vague notion. . . . The vagueness derives from the fluctuation of relative importance across contexts. We can resolve the vagueness if need be, by specifying which respects of comparison are important given our current concern."[24]

---

22. I thank Professor Michael Smith for helping me to see these subtle differences between Hume and Stout. Personal communication, September 1, 2005.

23. Goodman, "Seven Strictures on Similarity," 13–22; Goodman, *Ways of Worldmaking*.

24. Stout, *Democracy and Tradition*, 228.

Hopefully, what I have done in this chapter is not arbitrary and vague but demonstrates that there are genuine similarities between Hume's and Stout's pattern of reasoning. I will show that Stout's work bears marks of subterranean influence of Hume, if not an open and direct one. Whether such similarities that we can show are direct or not, I do not think is very important. My assumption and what I take as important is that it is the nature of the problem they were both trying to solve that led them to the "same" structure of answer, similar algorithm. This is not altogether new in the academic world and especially in the field of computer architecture and software development. Now let me state that I cannot prove that Stout was consciously aware of Hume's pattern of reasoning when he did his own work, nor can I provide a direct confirmation of my assumption. What we have here is only a hypothesis. If it explains the connection between Hume's moral theory and that of Stout or shows the Humean foundation of Stout's public reason concept then it can be treated as a reasonable one.

It is now time to lay out what I regard as the architecture of Hume's and Stout's thought patterns. This effort is divided into four steps:

Step 1: The Task of Two Moral Theories

The purpose is to develop a standard for public evaluation or discourse that can either serve to adjudicate or focus conflicting viewpoints. Such is a standard we can use to regulate, revise, and correct our moral judgment or critique the views of others. Hume is concerned with the standard of moral taste or judgment. Stout is concerned with the standard of public debate or justified reason. The standard for accepting a reason as justified is that of a claim that is justified in the sense that no relevant reasons for doubting it remain standing within a given discursive context.

Step 2: The Approach

Both authors start with the full menu of sentiments or values in a given context. None is restrained from bringing his or her sentiments or religious commitments with them into the public sphere. There is no *a priori* dismissal of some viewpoints (especially religious ones) or sentiments as Rawls and Rorty did.

So in the third chapter of *Democracy and Tradition*, Stout rigorously argues that religious reasons and commitments have a place in the public

Methods of Ethical Analysis

exchange of reasons. He rejects Rawls's contractarian notion of public reason and Rorty's "commitments held in common" as unreasonable and undemocratic. On the whole, he rejects the notion of moral restraints in both cases and in their places accepts Hegel's dialectical normative expression. Religious reasons like any liberal or atheist's reasons are to be introduced into the process of public discursive exchange of reasons and political decision making. Everyone enters into discursive exchange with any point of view responsibly held. All that matters in discursive sociality is not any deontological requirement, but possibilities of expressive freedom.[25]

For Hume and Stout common morality in a given society is derived from sentiments or tradition respectively—and not from reason.[26] Which sentiments and what underwrite them to play in the public square? For Hume they are sentiments that are commonly shared and relate to our common humanity—what he calls sympathy, "sentiment of humanity." The moral distinctions that people make are derived from feelings of approbation or disapprobation. Commonly shared democratic tradition is the main underwriter for Stout.[27] Stout's book could be reasonably read as a theory about how the origin and sustenance of our basic moral concepts, distinctions, and responsibility to one another lie in our democratic tradition of discursive exchange—note his discussions on ethics without metaphysics and ethics as social practice. Common morality does not derive from rational *a priori* principles or innate ideas but from practice. The overall discussions in the book indicate that the ability to grasp the importance and the place of exchange of reasons as the basis of public policies requires

---

25. Ibid., 67–68, 78–80, 82–84.

26. See *Treatise*, 457, 468–69 for Humean view. See also Radcliffe, "Hume on Motivating Sentiments," 40–41. If the meaning of reason is expanded as Annette Baier did in her book, *A Progress of Sentiments*, then this statement becomes shaky. Baier enlarged the Humean account of reason in the last chapter of her book. "One of the ways in which the *Treatise* presents a progression of thought, according to Baier, is in the turn from narrow conception of reason as the activity of solitary intellects to a broader vision of reason a virtuous trait of passionate and social beings." McIntyre, "Norms for a Reflective Naturalist," 321.

27. Stout, *Democracy and Tradition*, 78–80. One can conceivably argue that Stout's theory is based on reason insofar as one holds that all moral norms reduce to norms of reason and rationality. But I do not think that he has this in mind because it will be that in the end his moral theory is a form of consequentialism and therefore raises the issue of why benefits accruing to the majority in the society are not better than "public reason" that may or may not favor the majority group. (For how moral theories can be boiled down to forms of consequentialism see Smith, *Meta-Ethics*; Dreier, "Structures of Normative Theories," 22–40.

the possession of appropriate sentiments, piety, and dispositions toward the democratic tradition. Besides, the discussions also suggest that thoughts of continuing our ethical inheritance or cherished democratic tradition may itself motivate us and in this sense the ground of morality could be taken to be as internal to the agent as in the Humean scheme. All this does not mean that Stout's theory of morality precludes comparison of ideas or reasoning about matters of fact.

There is another move both authors have to make once they have gone down this route of all sentiments being entitled and free to play in the public square. The working of sympathy is variable and Hume argues it should not reflect on moral judgment in that form. Hume is not saying people should disregard or ignore their sentiments or personal interests but they should control them in making moral judgment. The conception of public reason that Stout is concerned with also has to deal with the issue of control. He says, for example, if a person favors a particular public policy and cites religious reasons for her position, she has to take seriously the objections raised against her premises and make a concerted attempt to give reasons why others must accept her conclusion—of course, this reason must be justified in the sense Stout defined justification.

I think it is for the purpose of developing the nuance between accepting every sentiment into play and yet wanting to arrive at a "public reason" (the whole movement from private to public reason) that Stout strenuously labored to make the distinction he made between being justified in believing something ("in the sense of being entitled to believe it") and being able to justify a claim to someone else ("in the sense of producing an argument that successfully undermines someone's relevant reasons for doubting it").[28]

His discussions of specific theologians and of scholarly counterarguments make room for him to clarify the need for the necessary transition from private (from believe what you want and it is your business) to public reason (to the belief that the larger community will accept as long as it is not succumbing to Hobbesian or thirty-years' war techniques). His trenchant critique of John Milbank, Alasdair McIntyre, and Stanley Hauerwas, and his theory of secularism are to establish and drum home the fact that there are contradictions in the exchange of reasons or sentiments in the public. The contradictions cannot be removed by highhandedness because America is a democracy, nor can they be reconciled by sectarian withdrawal behind fortified embankments because all citizens need to live harmoniously

---

28. Stout, *Democracy and Tradition*, 247.

Methods of Ethical Analysis

with one another. It is only by dialectical exchange of reasons where all are open to "novel performances" and their attendant consequences of transformation of normative concepts that a democratic community can arrive at justifiable public reason.

Step 3: The Standard of Taste or "Point of View of a Citizen"

Once Hume and Stout are embarked on the route of Steps 1 and 2 above, the logical thing to do is to seek a standard that can possibly solve the problems of variability and contradictions of sentiments without rejecting sentiment's role. As Hume argues, once a man makes a public statement, though he is expressing his sentiments, he expects all in his audience to concur with him. "He must here, therefore, depart from his private and particular situation, and must choose a point of view, common to him with others; he must choose some universal principle of the human frame, and touch a string to which all mankind have an accord and symphony."[29]

Public reason or moral judgment should not remain parochial and variable as private reason or sympathy. Hume noted that our sympathies are affected by distance or contiguity and in this form are ill suited for making moral judgment[30] and making contribution to the welfare of others.[31] It is this need to control for fickleness and to search for a nonarbitrary way to separate right and wrong tastes—private and public reasons—that can command allegiance that drive both scholars to seek for a public standard.[32] So Hume says: "it is natural for us to seek a *Standard of Taste*; a rule, by which the various sentiments of men may be reconciled; at least, a decision, afforded, confirming one sentiment, and condemning another."[33]

So far we have learned that morality is grounded in sentiment or viewpoint. Such sentiment or viewpoint may have "reference to nothing beyond itself." If this assertion is true, how can a single standard be formed? Hume rejects the assertion as true, arguing that it would make the determination of common standard impossible and that in fact sentiments point to something beyond themselves.[34] Stout also rejects this kind of thinking

---

29. Hume, *Enquiries*, 272.
30. Ibid., 227, 230; Hume, *Treatise*, 581, 582.
31. Hume, *Enquiries*, 228, 584–85; Hume, *Treatise*, 585.
32. Hume, *Treatise*, 547n1; Hume, *Enquiries*, 272; Hume, "Standard of Taste," 229.
33. Hume, "Standard of Taste," 229.
34. Ibid., 229–30.

because it inevitably leads to absurd solipsism or unbounded relativity and ignores the salient role of virtues of piety, hope, and justice in the American democratic tradition and ethical life or in the inheritance of a people.[35] He believes that some claims are to be treated as having authority (albeit defeasible) by default and that discursive practices are not free-floating but guided by norms—even though they do not have foundations. He says:

> Consider any art, science, or sport you please. It should be clear that the norms of the practice at a given time constrain the behavior of those who participate in it by supplying them with reasons not to do certain things they are physically able to do. Behavior within the social practice is open to criticism in terms of the norms as they have come to be. But conformity to norms opens the possibility of novel performance, which have the dialectical potential to transform the practice, thus changing its norms.[36]

Given that both Hume and Stout reject relativity or notion of impossibility in reaching a common standard because of difference in sentiments, the issue is not to reject sentiments' or religious premises' role but to seek proper ways of regulating their influence that can properly account for the intersubjectivity of moral judgment or public reason. This is how the philosopher Geoffrey Sayre-McCord summarizes Hume's position on the intricate connection between sentiments and standards and I think it equally applies to the bridge Stout is building between private and public reasons in America's democratic tradition. "Our moral judgments, Hume holds, are usually, and are appropriately, guided not by how we individually feel at any given time, but instead by how we all would feel were we to take up a general point of view."[37] Stout wants the public reason not to depend on what a particular subculture's views are but how it will be if such views are appropriately situated in democratic public domain. Subscription to this value is indexed by a willingness of community members to engage in exchange of reasons and holding themselves responsible to act reasonably in the face of justified reasons.

---

35. Stout, *Democracy and Tradition*, 5–15, 19–41, 212–13, 238–40.
36. Ibid., 79.
37. Sayre-McCord, "Why Hume's 'General Point of View,'" 209.

Methods of Ethical Analysis

Step 4: The Problem of Justification of the Standard of Taste

I have so far shown that the similarity in the tasks Hume and Stout set out to tackle has imposed certain constraints and suggested specific moves toward solutions. The tasks appear to be similar, the invitation to public reason is cut from the same cloth (all sentiments and premises are allowed into moral judgment), the approaches resemble one another, and the solutions not only are alike but also make similar argumentative moves to secure their acceptance. The next and final area of similarity in the architecture of Hume's and Stout's moral theories is justification (or at least some aspect of it) given for their theories. What justifies the adoption of the standard propagated by either Hume or Stout? First, people in a community need to speak intelligibly to one another. Stout calls Americans to what he terms "the point of view of a citizen" and "to participate in the moral tradition of one's people, understood as civic nation."[38] He further states that "central to the democratic thought as I understand it is the idea of a body of citizens who reason with one another about the ethical issues that divide them, especially when deliberating on the justice or decency of political arrangements."[39] Hume also seeks justification in the need for a society to live harmoniously.[40] Second, as Hume argues the adoption of a general point of view rather than a parochial one helps to mitigate continual contradictions as each speaks from his own point of view. Why are contradictions or differences problematic for Hume and Stout? In recognizing that our disagreements or agreements in society "play a distinctive and profound role not simply in how we treat [people] . . . but also in shaping the lives we try, and try to get others, to live. . . . To the extent these sentiments prove unstable, unpredictable, and idiosyncratic, and to the extent they conflict, so too will the plans and projects we and others undertake at their prodding."[41] Stout is concerned that without some agreement, some conception of public reason that adequately recognizes pluralism, democracy is threatened in America. "There is some danger . . . that a dualistic picture of our cultural situation, if accepted by enough people, will *become* true. To the extent that believers and nonbelievers accept the caricatures and exclusive choices now

---

38. Stout, *Democracy and Tradition*, 5.
39. Ibid., 6.
40. Hume, *Treatise*, 581–82.
41. Sayre-McCord, "Why Hume's 'General Point of View,'" 217.

on offer, they become more likely to retreat into separate camps that are incapable of reasoning and living peaceably with one another."[42]

By way of reaching conclusion on what for lack of a better word I have called, "the architecture of Hume and Stout theories of morality," I would like to state the aims of their theories. This may lend further credibility to my attempt to lay bare the similarity in their thoughts. As Sayre-McCord has argued, Hume's moral theory aims to provide an explanation of morality in terms of articulating the principles of morality.[43] This is also the primary task of Stout, as is evidenced in his grappling with his conception of public reason. Both Hume and Stout attempt to also give a sense of the purpose served by morality; they are not satisfied with merely explaining but also want to justify it.

In the following section, I will examine similarities in even the ambivalences of both authors in putting forward the explanation and justificatory tasks of their theories. Hume's moral theory oscillates between (or holds in tension) utilitarianism and contractarianism. Stout's theory of public reason verges at the edge of pragmatism and *democratic traditionalism*. Is there anything in the nature of the tasks they undertook or the shared architecture of their arguments that might just account for the ambiguities? I argue below that both of them attempt to offer alternatives to two opposing views, as steering a course between them, but are often not successful as their views often collapse into one or the other.

Section Three: Ambivalences in Moral Theories

I will start with Stout's pragmatic-expressivism to illustrate the ambivalences in the theories. Pragmatic-expressivism or *democratic traditionalism* is "an attempt to bring the notions of democratic deliberation and tradition together in a single philosophical vision."[44] "I am trying to articulate a form of pluralism, one that citizens with strong religious commitments can accept and that welcomes their full participation in public life without fudging on its premises."[45] This project is one of the immediate goals of the book but the way he has developed his arguments leaves lots of ambiguity and ambivalence. What does he mean by "fudging on its premises"? Reli-

---

42. Stout, *Democracy and Tradition*, 10; italics in the original.
43. Sayre-McCord, "Why Hume's 'General Point of View,'" 203–4.
44. Stout, *Democracy and Tradition*, 13.
45. Ibid., 296–97.

gious citizens are welcome in the public square but they or their theological convictions are not to "fudge on its premises"? I suppose not to "fudge on its premises" means believers must subject their religious reasons to "public reason" which he conceives as higher—public reasons are those that can only be justified (by the import of his definition) and they are justified not on appeal to a higher being or authoritative text. Religious reason is one mere reason among many that come into dialogue in a community with diverse convictions. So he is asking religious citizens to enter the public sphere without their cherished loyalties. In this regard he posits a gap between justification and truth and between justified in holding a belief and justification of a belief. The reason for positing such a gap is to foster a spirit of self-criticism and open-ended inquiry. What is he really getting at by all this? Those with theological convictions should be humble about their claims of truth and thus should be tolerant while in a public democratic conversation.

Also for the sake of bringing religious traditionalism and democratic deliberation together, he claims to have formulated a non-relative, non-metaphysical concept of truth. On the one hand, he does aim to make room for theological claims, but on the other he rejects *a priori* the theological positions of some communities, such as Thomism and Anabaptism. His claim of a generous conception and non-metaphysical approach to truth notwithstanding, what he seems to have come up with is not open to theological positions and it is also in a sense metaphysical. He writes that "what we have agreed to do, in effect, is to treat truth in practice as something that cannot be settled simply by communal agreement. It is this underlying social agreement on the use of certain words in the process of self-criticism that gives the term 'true' its nonrelative sense."[46] One can thus regard the content of the "underlying social agreement" as a regulative ideal that is above community; if not, what does he mean by "cannot be settled by communal agreement"?

There is another ambiguity in Stout's explicit combination of pragmatism and traditionalism. He rolled in extensive discussions of virtues in his book to say that pragmatism or democracy is not against virtues or character formation that the traditionalists like Christian philosophers/theologians MacIntyre and Hauerwas regard as essential in passing on America's ethical inheritance to the next generation. But his discussion does not show that he really understands their position, or that of any other virtue ethicist

---

46. Ibid., 277.

for that matter. For MacIntyre and Hauerwas virtues come first and what is right to be done in a given situation is known by appealing to them. By contrast, Stout "tries to locate the virtues by first working out a criterion of right action [public reason-guided policies], and then investigate what sorts of personal characteristics best induce the right actions (or perhaps more accurately, to the good results)."[47]

Owing to Hume's well-known flirtation with utilitarianism, he too falls into this misunderstanding of virtue ethics. Both Hume and Stout "conceive of the relationship between virtue and right conduct in a manner that is different from virtue theorist and thus reject a central tenet of virtue ethics."[48]

While Stout explicitly combines democracy and traditionalism into "pragmatic-expressivism," Hume is not very clear on his merging of utilitarianism and contractarianism or even the affinities of his moral theory with them. Though Hume's, strictly speaking, is not utilitarianism as Sayre Mc-Cord has argued,[49] it veers very close to it.[50] Hume's theory also accommodates contractarian reading with his occasional appeal to self-interest and mutual benefit in explaining the usefulness of the general point of view.[51] Good moral solutions in the Humean view are recommended by appeals to both utilitarianism and contractarianism.[52]

My interest in identifying these ambivalences in both theories is to see if there is anything in the nature of the tasks they undertook or the common architecture of their arguments that might just account for the ambiguities. Indeed, there might just be one. Hume and Stout regard morality (virtues) as suited to solving some problem and at the same time to generating approval from anyone properly situated. According to Hume, "every quality of the mind is denominated virtuous, which gives pleasure by the mere survey; as every quality, which produces pain, is call'd vicious. This pleasure and this pain may arise from four different sources. For we reap a pleasure from the view of a character, which is naturally fitted to be useful to others, or to the person himself, or which is agreeable to others,

---

47. Dreier, "Structures of Normative Theories," 34.
48. I thank Professor Michael Smith for pointing out this nuanced understanding of Hume's and Stout's approach to virtue ethics.
49. Sayre-McCord, "Hume and the Bauhaus Theory," 280–98.
50. Hume, *Enquiries*, 180, 211, 212, 231, 279; Hume, *Treatise*, 578, 619.
51. Hume, *Treatise*, 581–82, 583, 602; Hume, *Enquiries*, 228, 272.
52. Sayre-McCord, "Hume and the Bauhaus Theory," 292.

Methods of Ethical Analysis

or to the person himself."[53] Needless to say that Stout lays out his theory as serving the purpose of bringing religious traditionalists and liberals into a democratic conversation. As he puts it, he has set out to chart an "acceptable path between the liberalism of Rawls and Rorty, on one hand, and the traditionalism of MacIntyre and Hauerwas on the other."[54] The prospect of his ethical theory securing either group's approbation hangs on the groups being moved by the theory's touted benefit for the "civic nation." At the same time, his appeal to groups "like the Christian majority who have half-acknowledged democratic commitments" to be committed to the civic nation is really an attempt to secure their approval of his proposal based on benefits others will receive from it. The appeal of his proposal is not based on benefits to all who might be affected by it. His is not an appeal to maximizing overall utility. The Christians who are in majority and who have to shed some of their "theological clothes" and loyalties in the public square stand to lose more than any group under his theory. This works like the obligation the strong has to the weak in Hume's view of virtue of justice. The strong may not have self-interested reason to extend justice to the weak or harbor an expectation of mutual advantage but do so because they are bound by the laws of humanity to give justice to the weak even if the weak cannot make them feel the effect of their resentment.[55] In the case of Stout, the majority group is bound by the norms of democracy to yield to the use of public reason in policy formulation.

Section Four: Affinities, Differences, and Problems

In the preceding three sections, I have argued that Stout's conception of public reason has affinities with Hume's moral theory. This is not to say they are identical in the architecture of their arguments or to deny crucial differences between the two. Not the least of which is the role of general point of view and public reason under the two programs. In Hume's account it is central that people take up the general point of view, but he makes allowance for people to stay in their position of partiality and thus not insist that people must always take up the general point when dealing with personal matters, friends, or close ones. "In some cases, at least, remaining in one's position of partiality, say with respect to one's family and friends or oneself,

53. Hume, *Treatise*, 591.
54. Stout, *Democracy and Tradition*, 296.
55. Hume, *Enquiries*, 190.

is appropriate and would itself secure the approval of those who do occupy the general point of view. It is not part of Hume's theory that we should always take up the general point of view in facing the world...."[56] For Stout, public reason once justified is what rules in all cases.[57] Though the public reasons offered in each case of public policy may differ, it is public reason in the broad sense that rules. In the discursive community there should be no going back and forth on public and private reason, between public and private standard.

This strict place given to public reason by Stout raises very thorny issues. This strictness introduces what I will call a backdoor deontological feature into what at first sight appears to be an expressive, pragmatic, or democratic traditionalist theory.[58] There are two reasons for this view. First, once this public reason emerges from the college of debaters, as a cardinal emerges as pope from a conclave of cardinals, it becomes one's duty to obey and it implies, all things considered, one should do it. Public reason once arrived at cannot be overridden or outweighed. It is a trump over any other justification that any person, group, institution, or government may have over any public action. It looks like a side-constraint that restricts both what citizens may take as their public policy goals and how they may go about implementing them. Stout is silent or not clear on which occasions it will be better to violate his rule of public reason. By his neat and strict conception of the proper place of public reason in discursive exchanges there is no room for a disjunctive conception of duty demanded by public reason or moral permission to act "above or below the line of duty,"[59] or acknowledge that there may be occasions when "morality may not be rationally overriding."[60] Second, the right-making features in Stout's ethical theory are not only those that are picked out by agent-neutral "public

---

56. Sayre-McCord, "Why Hume's 'General Point of View,'" 222. See Kathleen Wallace, who also argues that "universality" or intersubjective agreement in Hume's moral theory is "sensitive to social context and allows for variation in where the line is drawn, so to speak." Wallace, "Hume on Regulating Belief," 93.

57. He even defined the public to include a gathering of three citizens. *Democracy and Tradition*, 113.

58. Perhaps, stating that he brought in a deontological feature through the backdoor is not an apt characterization. By his emphasis on giving and evaluation of reasons and holding people responsible or accountable for their actions in a democratic society he has all along had an implicit Moorean notion of the deontic in view: *best outcome* and *capacity* or *option*.

59. Wolf, "Above and Below," 131–48.

60. Wolf, "Meaning and Morality," 311.

reason," but also it is the reason we can all reasonably agree to serve as the directive of public policy. But what should we care for Stout's conception of public reason that precludes agent-relative permissions and commitments to exclusive personal love and friendships? In other words what is the normativity of his public reason claim? How can he explain why his proposal deserves to be given a special significance in our decisions and choices? Why must "public reason" have an overriding authoritative reason for decision in the public sphere?

At first blush, given that public reason is what serves as basis of agreement or what can only be (as per his definition) justified, it is perhaps proper to state that the normative significance of his theory resides in the actual agreement or acceptance. But I am sure Stout will reject this. Several places in his book he states what is important is "what kind of people we are going to be—a matter of self-identity and integrity."[61] So it appears that the source of normativity is in some practical identity as a conception of the American self under which all must value themselves. And the identity in view here is the democratic identity that has endured for generations. National values are embedded in such an identity. Here we see one reason why Stout spent so much time in delineating, describing, and explaining America's democratic tradition. He was looking for a place to ground the public-reason standard in a way that does not appear arbitrary, and "to show that it has a status in virtue of which it is relevantly 'authoritative' or 'normative.'"[62] While religious citizens may accept justifying themselves to others for the sake of living in a mutually dependent community or for some national identity in ordinary circumstances, it is not clear why they should in "circumstances in which being moral would leave them shattered as to be perhaps without any further reason to live at all"?[63] For many their lives will be going worse if they were not acting on their true beliefs (what gives meaning to their lives) but acquiescing to "public reason."

Beyond the issue of normativity there is a more immediate practical problem. Stout's insistence that it is public reason and public reason alone that has a place in the public square and unlike Hume, his unfaltering commitment to it, means that those who do not share his view but still want to participate in policy formulation will have to become Susan Wolf's "moral

---

61. Stout, *Democracy and Tradition*, 200.

62. For a good discussion on normativity of standards see Copp, "Normativity of Self-Grounded Reason," 40.

63. Wolf, "Meaning and Morality," 311.

saints." Wolf amply argues that this is not an admirable venture many persons want to undertake.[64] As George Orwell writes:

> sainthood is . . . a thing that human beings must avoid . . . It is too readily assumed that . . . ordinary man only rejects it because it is too difficult; in other words, that the average human being is a failed saint. It is doubtful whether this is true. Many people genuinely do not wish to be saints, and it is probable that some who achieve or aspire to sainthood have never felt much temptation to be human beings.[65]

Besides, many may find the idea of public reason just too demanding, asking them to make a sacrifice that entails giving up their very reason for living, losing the meaning of life. As Bernard Williams puts it: "there can come a point at which it is quite unreasonable for a man to give up, in the name of the impartial good ordering of the world of moral agents, something which is a condition of his having any interest in being around in that world at all."[66] If because of increasing secularization, pluralism, traditionalism, or for whatever reason democracy becomes too demanding or conflicting, many citizens may not find in it an engaging and worthwhile project.[67] Stout's theory appears to be too demanding because his conceptions of democracy and public reason do not relate to what gives meaning to people's lives and not just happiness. What gives a person a reason to live or a reason to care about anything in the world is often different from the reason to enter into discursive exchange with fellow countrypersons to generate "public reasons" for public policies. If past public reasons have emptied a person's life of meaning or if prospective public reason is going to do just that it would not make sense for a citizen to go out and participate in generating more public reasons.[68]

The main focus of this section has been the implications of the strictness Stout attaches to his conception of public reason as compared to the relative flexibility Hume's general point of view allows. There is one more angle to explore the implications of Stout's strictness. The strictness fails

64. Wolf, "Moral Saints," 419–39.

65. Orwell, "Reflection on Gandhi," 176, quoted in Wolf, "Moral Saints," 436.

66. Williams, "Persons, Character and Morality," 14, quoted in Wolf, "Meaning and Morality," 299–300.

67. For a discussion on how engagement in projects of worth secures meaning in people's lives see Wolf, "Happiness and Meaning," 207–25.

68. Wolf, "Meaning and Morality," 305–8.

to properly acknowledge the dynamics of public reason. If Stout was not thinking of public reason as something that emerges in one sitting in a town's hall, then I find as problematic his failure to examine how "unspecified obligations, uncertain time horizons, and the possible violations of reciprocity expectations"[69] affect the emergence and evolution of public reason, which I imagine is a social capital. As a social capital, public reason is a by-product of other social activities and is subject to the dilemma of collective action.[70] If his idea of the discursive exchange is not modeled on stock market exchange he must account not only for its less transparency, more uncertainty, and less credible mutual commitments, but also to its dynamics relative to economic exchange.

The need to clarify the dynamics is not satisfied by just stating that public reasons emerge from discursive exchange. The notion that in a free discursive exchange, public policy will rise to the level dictated by public reason ignores the common observation that no public reason travels the road to the top entirely alone. The social context within which ideas and private reasons emerge and mature strongly condition their transformation into public reasons and give them dynamics all of their own relative to economic exchange. This implies that strict adherence to public reason without making allowance for other considerations as Hume did with his general point of view is an ideal that demands too much. Every thorough going theory of public reason must take into account these three decomposable parts: the social relationships that make the exchange of private reasons possible and breathe (public reason inheres in social structures, not in policy documents), the nature and breadth (range of acceptability) of the emergent public reason, and an "ethics of human dignity," which shows how citizens should treat and relate to one another. Stout in his book concerns himself only with some of the formal aspects of the breadth and ethics.

Section Five: Concluding Remarks

In closing, I would like to emphasize the modesty of my attempt to identify the commonly shared architecture of arguments in both Hume's and Stout's moral theories. I have at best identified affinities between both theories and pointed out a crucial difference; all along believing that I would be able to

---

69. Portes, "Social Capital," 4.
70. Putnam, "Prosperous Community," 35–42.

Jeffrey Stout's Theory of Public Reason

let the reader see the shared ordered structure beneath the flow of philosophical language and arguments.

These are some of the striking similarities between Hume's moral theory and Stout's theory of public reason:

(a) Both require that individuals enter the discursive exchange or start the moral evaluation process with all their sentiments, values, or premises.

(b) Both require that sentiments or values (private reasons) be corrected to fall in line with those of fellow citizens. That is, each person steps away from his or her peculiar viewpoint and takes up a shared general point of view. This is to reduce or eliminate contradictions. "Instead of independent votes, we have verdicts reached after full discussion and attempted persuasion."[71] The general point of view corrects the "output from sympathy" and objective public reason corrects output from private reasons.

(c) The audience for whom sentiments and values are to be appropriately corrected is a narrow one. Both use the notion of a narrow circle because for them objectivity (which is the stepping out of peculiar standpoint to the general standpoint) is somewhat context-dependent.

(d) The all-important general point of view or the public reason is not from nowhere but from the common membership in the "party of humankind" (served with an inborn mechanism of sympathy) or from democratic tradition.

(e) The subject matters on which this shared viewpoint is to be exercised are limited to public or common good.

I am not the first person to find similarities between Hume's general point of view and that of another philosopher. Baier identified about the same set of striking similarities between Hume's version of the point of view and the version of the general will given by Jean-Jacques Rousseau.[72] As a matter of fact when I told Stout that I had found striking similarities between his conception of the public reason and Hume's moral theory he referred me to Baier's book on Hume's *Treatise* as his favorite work on Hume.[73]

71. Baier, *Progress of Sentiments*, 183.
72. Ibid., 182–83.
73. I wish to state that before Stout showed me Baier's book I was not aware of the

61

Methods of Ethical Analysis

Overall, this chapter has helped us to understand the important role the conception of public reason plays in ethical debates. Needless to say that this chapter makes explicit the nature of debates surrounding public reason, which chapter 1 glosses over. The ethical methodology discussed in chapter 1 represents a commitment to public exchange of reasons in democratic pluralistic communities. In such communities there are (or ought to be) standards for accepting reasons or claims for public policy. What are these standards in the United States? Or how can we formulate and evaluate them? The demand to grapple with this kind of pertinent questions that must inform the ethical methodology is what drove us to work of Jeffrey Stout. We turn to the work of public theologian Max Stackhouse in the next chapter to examine how to interpret public debates about globalization, which might start from the sentiments and religious premises of a theological conception of *New Jerusalem*.

---

connection she pointed out between Hume and Rousseau. I left reading her book until I came to writing the conclusion of this essay.

CHAPTER THREE

Max Stackhouse: Globalization and Theology of History

Opening Word

MAX STACKHOUSE BELIEVES THAT ethics must be situated or undergirded by the theological contemplation of the panorama of history. He argues that history is moving toward a goal, the realization of the universal common, the global civil society, the *New Jerusalem*. The focus of his work as interpreted in this chapter is to work out the logic of history and from the logic of history derive an objectively valid value system, the standards to judge different religions and social systems, and to guide the emerging global civil society; precisely, theological ethics must craft the system of values and religious symbols to guide its proper functioning. His ethical methodology is deeply penetrated by a philosophy or theology of history.

Why this emphasis on religious interpretation of history as the inner logic of ethical methodology? He argues that all civilizations have two sides that come together in existence and cease to be at the same time. There is always the visible, material side to every civilization and has as its counterpart, the invisible, inner spirit, driving energy, spiritualism, intellectual, and convictional structures. Religion defines this inner spirit and it is the primary factor in shaping the common life; religion as an independent variable interacts with material interests to shape economies. He argues that no civilization in the past has been formed and sustained without a religious core, without theology/mythology and ethics sustaining it. Is religion necessary to guide the emerging global civilization? If yes, what should be the religious core of the emerging global civilization? Stackhouse developed his theology of globalization in a vigorous attempt to address this question.

Methods of Ethical Analysis

Chapter Introduction

Stackhouse is widely known in many circles for his work in public theology, globalization, human rights, family life, and the moral basis of business life, but not for his theology of history.[1] Yet, all of these are rooted in his theology of history. The interpretation of history is the central problem of Stackhouse's theology, ethics, and philosophy. His theology of history is based on a theistic interpretation of the changing dynamics and structures of society in which religion plays a critical role. According to him, the church, as the "mother" of a new and decisive kind of social institution beyond kinship, class, and state, is the turning point in history in the West and increasingly around the world; and it is that which potentially could lead history toward its fulfillment, as inspired by the eschatological promise of the *New Jerusalem*, an urban, cosmopolitan civilization, a global civil society or association of voluntary societies.

For Stackhouse, globalization is a civilizational shift that reflects the universalizing of certain biblical insights made concrete in social life in the context of many cultures—the result of which is a new economic interdependence. He also view globalization as a providential process that is leading humanity to their global civil society. In this journey the church is the originary image of globalization's future, and it is also an instrument of godly intent, creating a new public that could lead globalization's future.

The turning point that shifted history toward globalization is the appearance of the church (a *novum*) and it can potentially lead history to its approximate fulfillment, not because of any special virtues of the church (though these are not rejected), but because of its historical function. This function is nothing but the movement toward the New Jerusalem, a global civil society. With the emerging global civil society—which is generated by globalization—we are now not only better understanding this function, but we are also better placed to see the center in which the meaning of history appears. His theology of globalization is a method of gesturing to the summarizing characterization of the polyform ways the global civil society is being realized and as identifying the general principle of history.[2] The

---

1. Consider this quote, for instance: "Of particular importance for modern business is the idea that there is an ultimate end for humanity beyond death, and that the vision of the end is the New Jerusalem, a cosmopolitan and complex urban civilization into which all the peoples of the earth can bring their gifts. *This is the key to a theology of history*." Stackhouse, "Signs of Hope"; italics in the original.

2. Before the current globalization the corporation (as *corpus Christi*: such as the

creation of civil society, an ecclesia (a consocation of incorporated bodies) that transcends biophysical and narrow political alliances is the general principle of history. Put another way, the spiritual movement toward the New Jerusalem is the dynamic power of history; and global civil society is the earthly approximation of New Jerusalem.

The best entry into Stackhouse's unified and complex theology of globalization and history is his notion of ecclesia, a *universal common,* and what is shared in it. What is shared in the common is pneuma and freedom. Stackhouse casts his theology of history as the universal move of the Holy Spirit, with the church as a new instrument of godly intent, creating a new public that could approximate the New Jerusalem, a global urban city. In this interpretation of the church as a global urban city and civilization (a universal space of freedom) and as the catholic gathering of all of God's children under the Spirit's directionality, Stackhouse makes a nuanced adjustment to the theology of the church. For instance, whereas Paul gave universal validity to the ecclesia by according citizenship in it only on the basis of *pistis* (faith in Christ), Stackhouse gives universal validity to his "global civil ecclesia" via faith in the ideals of the Judeo-Christian worldview. He believes that the Judeo-Christian worldview can move freedom and justice from the *particular* (local, ethnic, national, cultural sensibilities and allegiance) into the global, universal common space opened up by globalization.

It important to add that for Stackhouse, ecclesia refers both to the church and the expanded notion of New Jerusalem as a deterritorialized global urban city and civilization. The two sense of the word is founded on the notion of an *in-between* space. The church as well as the New Jerusalem is a social space between persons/groups and the political state, and between nation-states. It is space both in the physical and social senses. In his complex and nuanced usage of the term, it also carries spatial and historical meanings. It is obviously a social space, and something more: a moving force of history. This kind of space, according to him, only emerged at a certain point in Western Christian history and it will be historically fulfilled in the New Jerusalem.[3]

---

university, the monastery, the "free city," and chartered business) had also emerged as an ecclesia. See Stackhouse, "New Moral Context," 239–53; Stackhouse, "Moral Roots," 29–39.

3. Stackhouse's theology of history and globalization embeds an interesting perspective on the relationship between time and space. Though time dominates over space because the events in his narratives are moving toward a new epoch (the New Jerusalem), space itself is de-territorialized. The New Jerusalem is not a physical space, but

Methods of Ethical Analysis

The historical function of the church, he insists, can only be adequately understood when the church is properly seen as an *ecclesia*, a body of people called out of ordinary life to form an urban assembly; as a space between the family (blood, biology) and the state (politics), the two prime units of society which requires also an economy, culture, and religion. In Western society the church created that in-between space that was not beholden to biology (tribes, ethnicity, tribes, clans, caste or endogamous units) and to the state (political authority, legitimate power in a territory).[4] It called persons to a new identity and a social space that was in-between these two poles. Today, globalization is creating a civil society, a space between nations; a consociation of voluntary associations, which creates a social space not subject to blood, race, ethnicity (genetic connection), special interest or central political control by force. This global, deterritorialized rhizomatic space between nations, he has named the New Jerusalem.

In Stackhouse's thinking the Christian church as the originator of civil society also constitutes the ideal of all civil societies, which are various forms of ecclesia insofar as they occupy an in-between space between the family and the state. The church (the non-institutional, non-absolutizing church) as the original civil society in the West is the one form of ecclesia that has the power to critique and lead all civil societies and the emerging global commons to their ideal form, the New Jerusalem.

---

rhizomatic networks of civilizations and cultures that have no center. It is an in-between, a *commons*.

4. He argues:
    Historically, the founding and formation of the church nurtured a new and decisive kind of institution beyond regime, kinship, and class. From Paul on, the mission of the church was the reorganization of responsible freedom and the recentering of associational loyalty as well as the creation of social organizations little known in the pagan world. It was the formation of a covenanted ecclesia of worship and service, defined by a religious worldview based in faith in Jesus Christ and in the sovereignty of the Triune God. This is the mother of civil society, until recently seldom acknowledged by social theorists or political scientists, but today accented in new studies of the relationship of the world religions to democracy. This social novum established a new sense of identity and gradually created new social spaces to form and reform other human associations that, over time, became not only the congregation and monastery but also the university, the hospital, the council, the corporation, and the professional associations that nurtured accountable vocations dedicated to incarnating a divinely-given ethic in these organs of the common ethos, as has been traced by historians of law. From these roots came the clusters of organizations and practices that are the indicators of a vibrant pre-political civil society. (Stackhouse, "Framing the Global Ethos," 8–9.)

Is Globalization a Unique Christian Gift to the World?

Why the privileging of the Christian church as the basis of understanding history and interpreting the forces of globalization? Stackhouse argues that he has chosen Christianity as the focal point for the analysis of history and globalization not because there is something supremely unique to it but it alone has the right combination of protest (critique), creation (transformation), and the eschatological vision of new creation to support the emerging forces and it alone has the non-exclusionary tendency to accommodate all in equal terms under one tent. Christianity also rejects the idea that the family or race, the political order or the state, the economy or culture are the absolute center of meaning, loyalty or salvation. The Christian church is the true *ecclesia*, assembly of God's people such that the basis of belonging to it is not blood, race, caste, nationality, or reason, but by grace all have equally received from God. As Paul Tillich, Stackhouse's teacher once put it:

> [Membership in the ecclesia] is not a matter of race or of reason. It is a matter of historical destiny. . . . The church is *one* historical reality starting with the promise of God to Abraham, centered in the appearance of Christ, and moving forward to the final fulfillment. The spatial ecclesia of Greece [and earlier forms of ecclesia] has [have] been replaced by the *historical* ecclesia of Christianity, the bearer of historical consciousness in all periods and nations.[5]

Stackhouse believes that the vision of the church as the true ecclesia can only be realized in a globalized world. The true ecclesia is the globalized world in which tribal identities and minor religious affiliations, class loyalties or narrow statehoods have been conquered in principle and the kingdom of God established.

As stated earlier, the best way to understand Stackhouse's controversial thesis is to understand his notion of ecclesia as a theory of the universal common. His problematic privileging of Christianity as a unique force of history is mainly based on his understanding of ecclesia and its emergence as a civil society in the West. The organizing principle of Stackhouse's theology of history and globalization is his theory of common (public) space or ecclesia based on a covenantal understanding of social and personal relationships in societies.

According to this writer's interpretation the bulk of this thought— from his understanding of social ethics, church, human rights, religion,

---

5. Tillich, *Protestant Era*, 31.

corporations, and to his conceptualization of globalization—he has been concerned with how protected social spaces were created in history, how new ones can be created, what ethos should determine their operations, and what should be their ultimate trajectory. For example, when he writes about human rights in his book, *Creeds, Society and Human Rights*, he argues that part of the ethos of human rights is voluntary institutions that inhere in a distinctive and protected social space.[6] These are institutions that are between family/ethnic and the state. These voluntary organizations and the space within which they exist were pioneered by the church tradition in the West. The existence of this space was taken as a human right: political authority does not grant "concessions" (that is, civil rights granted by civil authority). The community (the *common*) is prior to and even distinct from the political solidarity or state. The church operated from this social space and pressed every sector to resist absolutizing itself—arguing that no human being or human institution can have the place of ultimate authority. It was also from this protected space that the church nudged all social institutions toward transformation.

This is a historic role he assigns only to Christianity and going further to assert that it is only a Christian understanding of ecclesia that can guide the emerging global civil society. Islam and Hinduism, he argues, failed to properly create a distinctive social space that could protect universal human rights or function as a civil society. The notion of emerging global society or universal human rights demand not only a social space for universalistic oriented associations in society, separated from tribal, class or political consideration or loyalties, but also a universal understanding of humanity. The political theology of Islam rejects free space between the family/ethnic and the state and attempts to bring all human associations under the rubric of a theocratic state. The problem here is that the Islamist political theology "lauds a politically comprehending, sacred regime that has a duty to rule over all other groups and institutions, with the patriarchal family being the 'natural' microcosm of the larger political form. This implies a political theory of society [rather than a social theory of politics]."[7] This is a criticism he also levies against some Christian Fundamentalist views, fascism, and communism.

Hinduism because of the caste system cannot create a distinctive, common social space that transcends blood or gene pool. Its common

---

6. Stackhouse, *Creeds, Society and Human Rights*.
7. Stackhouse, "Framing the Global Ethos," 8.

space is not truly gene neutral and cross cutting, or voluntaristic and pluralistic. Ideas of Hinduism on their own do not support the creation of communities of persons with equal standing. What it means to be human in Hinduism does not support a universal understanding of humanity—except at one level, *atman*.

The questions Stackhouse poses here for theology are these: What conception of being human is universal enough to accommodate the emerging global civilization? What kind of social patterns can support beliefs and actions on universal values; go beyond racial, gender, class, and ethnic ideologies? Which of the world religions can supply us with the theology to help guide the emerging global civil society toward equality, justice, and universal human rights? Which of them should (can) form the *convictional center* of the emerging global society? Answering these questions is for him the urgent and central theological challenge of our age. He writes:

> Since no enduring civilization—indeed, no viable society within a civilization—has developed without a dominant religion at its core, and it is unlikely that a globalized civilization, or the structures of civil society likely to populate it, can develop in creative directions without one either, [thus] it makes a great difference which religion becomes dominant, how it does so, and how it treats other traditions.[8]

And thus for Christian theologian, the role of public theology (drawing its values and orientation principally from the Judeo-Christian worldview) is to define the proper ethos for the emerging global civilization. This task, he insists, begins with a Christianly theology of globalization. What is globalization?

Theology of Globalization

Here we will attempt to summarize Stackhouse's theology of globalization. As set out in his 2007 book, *Globalization and Grace*,[9] globalization is the potential emergence (emerging) of a global civil society—a complex, inclusive, urban, cosmopolitan civilization. It occupies the social space that is between nations. It is a space not beholden to bio-piety (gene pool) or geo-piety (to nations). According to him, we are experiencing the forma-

---

8. Stackhouse, "General Introduction," in Stackhouse and Paris, *God and Globalization*, 1:52.
9. Stackhouse, *Globalization and Grace*, Vol. 4.

tion of a new public, a worldwide civil society and possibly a new world civilization. We are participating in a process of potential civilizational shift that bears the prospect of a new form of civil society. He names the destiny of the process as New Jerusalem, a cosmopolitan and urban civilization. This emerging civilization has no center.

He maintains that the emerging global civilization is partly made possible by a growing acceptance of human rights, emancipation of women, democracy, fundamental equality of all persons, stewardship of the earth, and scientific rationality. These are values formed or legitimated by the Judeo-Christian worldview. The emerging global civil society is part of the evolutionary process of civil society started by the Church and furthered in many places by the missionary movement, which introduced (with colonialism) the modern corporation to many spheres of society. The Church and the modern corporation occupy the social space between the family and the state.

The modern corporation as a manifestation of the current globalization is also interpreted according to his theory of the ecclesia. Indeed, he maintains that the modern corporation is an ecclesia; a worldly ecclesia that is operating (should operate) under just laws and is accountable to society. The corporation is a cooperative human activity outside the family, tribe, government, and personal friendship. Its identity is not based on family or state, but based on the voluntary cooperation of owners and workers, producers and customers, and managers and stakeholders; collaborations based on transforming material reality. The major spheres of society are today organized as corporations: from education (universities), economy, entertainment and media, to healthcare (clinics and hospitals).

The modern corporation, as he put it, is like the Church in certain sociological respects. It is rooted in a form of covenant community, an association of interdependent persons seeking to produce goods and services for the common good. As such, he argues, theologians should overcome their contempt for this economic institution and see capital as serving people's needs and thus a "holy vocation in and for the salvation of world." They should work to guide corporations to the purpose of better serving the common good.[10] This interpretation of the modern corporation leads him to identify another dimension of the cosmopolitan social ethics that will address the emerging global civil society.

---

10. Stackhouse and McCann, "Postcommunist Manifesto," 949–54; Stackhouse, "Introduction" in Stackhouse and Obenchain, *God and Globalization*, 3:1–57.

> [T]heology adequate to the cosmopolitan challenges that await us must have another dimension as well: it must develop a social ethic of the emerging world in which democracy, human rights and a mixed economy are acknowledged as universal necessities. It must address a world linked by technology, trade, and a host of new interdependencies. This agenda for Christian thought requires a "public theology," a way of speaking about the reality of God and God's will for the world that is intellectually valid in the marketplace of ideas and morally effective in the marketplace of goods and services.[11]

Overall, Stackhouse understands globalization as a success in the historical Christian way of understanding the world. This Christian interpretation of history or way of being holds that history is not an eternal cycle and the goal of existence is not to escape the material world, but to engage it. Christians are to reconstruct the world aware of the tension between "the kingdom is here and it is yet to come." Globalization is only ambiguously the already and the not-yet. It is part of God's providential grace; and human beings and their governments cannot reverse "the tides of history at its deepest levels" but can influence its development.[12] Stackhouse states:

> We can understand that globalization involves error, destruction, and sin, but it also rests on and evolves good, reconstructing and transforming Grace—and thus it invites a vision that it anticipates in serious measure: an ultimate destiny symbolized as an inclusive heavenly city, the image of a complex and holy civilization which comes to us by grace. Globalization is, thus, a form of creational and providential grace coming to a catholic and ecumenical partial fulfillment that points us toward a salvific vision of humanity and the world. Those who grasp this vision may be called to become agents of God's reign in all areas of the common life, and channel all the powers of life toward the new possibilities.[13]

From the preceding paragraphs, we can discern that Stackhouse has a theology or philosophy of history that informs both this theory of ecclesia, the emerging global civil society, globalization a providential act of God, and his interpretation of the task of public theology. To this theology of history, we now turn.

---

11. Stackhouse and McCann, "Postcommunist Manifesto," 951.
12. Stackhouse, *God and Globalization*, 4:248.
13. Ibid., 4:249–50.

Methods of Ethical Analysis

An Overview of Stackhouse's Interpretation of History

Stackhouse's theology of history is the church (ecclesia) interpreted in terms of the spiritual impulses of history as the movement toward the New Jerusalem. The church, according to Stackhouse, is a bearer and manifestation of the Spirit of God in time and therefore is the perspective from which history ought to be interpreted. According to him, history can best be understood by tracing the structures and dynamics of social relations, institutions, and the forces (powers, principalities, authorities, and regencies) that shape them. These forces are differently shaped by dominions (religions). In this shaping process the Christian faith and the church have been decisive in the world.

For him, history is the metanarrative of the realization of the universal city through the common space (originated by the church or the Christian West) "inseminating itself globally"[14] or providentially unfolding itself. The oak tree that is the New Jerusalem is the maturity, blossoming, and fruition of the premodern Western Christian acorn.[15] In this replication of itself, this planting of the acorn (that is, the civil society, the common space in common cause with capitalism and Christian-originated Western values), Stackhouse invites us to consider this Western "originated" ecclesia as "the historically necessary and ontologically propitious globalization, not of its own particularity, but of the normative structures proper to the *nature of human existence as such*."[16]

Thusly, the subject matter of the historical science of civilization is the *Idee* of in-between, common space, that is, the concept of ecclesia together "with the actualization of that concept." The appointed role of public theology, the handmaiden of historical science (or philosophy/theology of history), is to elucidate the good, the right, and fitting personal, group, and institutional behaviors and responsibilities in the New Jerusalem (in its localized appearances; in its journey through deformed historical instantiations and toward universalism and deterritorialization) as the "actuality of concrete freedom," the "fulfillment of all humanity."

---

14. A borrowed phrase from Serequeberhan, *Contested Memory*, 15.

15. May I quickly add that we can follow Jean-Francois Lyotard to say that whenever the acorn appears, "it does not occur without shattering of belief, without a discovery of the *lack of reality* in reality—a discovery linked to the *invention* of other realities." See Lyotard, *Postmodern Explained*, 9, quoted in Serequeberhan, *Contested Memory*, 12; italics added.

16. Serequeberhan, *Contested Memory*, 12; italics in the original.

In this Max Stackhouse appears to be pointing to the church and the West (more precisely, Christianized West) as the future of the world. Karl Marx in 1867 wrote: "The country that is more developed industrially only shows, to the less developed, the image of its own future."[17] In Stackhouse's theory of history, the church is the *image* of globalization's own future. Nations are, he avers, moving toward "worldwide, federated civil society that will be decidedly dynamic, incredibly complex, and inevitably contentious . . . " and he quickly reminds us that the Church is "the mother of an independent civil society."[18] With the future clarified, the whole task of guiding globalization is how to subduct it under its originary image and worldview. If we know the image of the future, a singular future ("humanity's destiny is to be a New Jerusalem"[19]), then history is complete in principle.[20] In this already actualized future history has ended. Not that life will not go on, wars will not be fought, or businesses not compete against one another, it is only that we firmly know history's end and we are in the endgame of it. What really remains for us—ethicists, policymakers, and so on—is to work out the details, minimize pains, and reduce distortions in this already actualized future. In Stackhouse's theology of history and globalization we have a sophisticated theological version of Francis Fukuyama's end of history thesis!

Now wait a minute; what originary image do we really know or possess? What is the originary image that Stackhouse is asking us to draw from? It is the ideal one; the one which can never be distorted by the foibles of its inheritors and bearers in concrete lived experience. The image history itself cannot stain? Stackhouse in his 2009 presidential address to the American Theological Society stated that:

> The temptations of imperialism and colonialism can more accurately be seen as the results of those forms of debased Christian worldviews that have become separated from, or even contemptuous of, its deeper roots and ethical contours. . . . The hegemony that appears to be Americanism or capitalism gone wild is in fact a theologically decapitated set of vacuous cybernetic meanings.[21]

---

17. Marx, "Preface to the First Edition," 91.
18. Stackhouse, "Framing the Global Ethos," 4, 5.
19. Ibid., 7.
20. This paragraph inspired by Serequeberhan, *Contested Memory*, 107–9.
21. Stackhouse, "Framing the Global Ethos," 5.

Methods of Ethical Analysis

So what is the Church; what is the *eidos*? The Church is both a historic formation and universal model that no historical eventuations of concrete existence can despoil. Has Stackhouse here ontologized the ontic manifestations of a particular history (church history, European history)? This unanswered questions form, at least, part of the backdrop to his understanding of the role of public theology or social ethics in a globalizing.

Intersection of Public Theology and Globalization

Stackhouse identifies the major role of public theology as in the structuring of the emerging global civil society, the global ecclesia. The role of theology (theological ethics) is threefold: first, theological ethics must evaluate the ethos (operating values, norms and expectations) as needed to make the right and good movements into the New Jerusalem—the ultimate vision that bends in on the present. This ethos must be such that it invites all to become participants in a global civil society. He writes:

> In the past, theology played a major role in shaping the principles that were to guide the encounter and clash of societies, although such concerns have not been central to theology for generations. What ought we do when we face the creation of a world society that presents us with a common future without a common past?[22]

Second, theological ethics must develop an approach rooted in a worldview(s) that can channel life and life powers (mars, muses, eros, mammon, and so on) toward the future in this emerging global space.[23]

---

22. Stackhouse, "Social Theory," 40.

23. See Stackhouse, *God and Globalization*, 4:158. See also Stackhouse, "Introduction" in Stackhouse and Paris, *God and Globalization*, 1:35. There are five major spheres of society or "orders of creation" in any civilization: family, polity, culture, economy, and religion. (Each of these spheres has its associated *principalities*: family [eros], polity [mars], culture [muses], economy [mammon], and religion [dominion]). Each needs its own social space to develop. Each sphere needs a significant degree of freedom from state (external) control in order to support human flourishing and influence the political order. These spheres are institutionalized patterns to house and guide the biological and socio-physical energies: the dynamic spiritual forces that invite and capture people's loyalties and shape the ethos of societies. These not only enable people to move beyond the boundaries and capabilities left to them by their ancestors, but can also, and too often, anchor them to antiquated practices, institutions, and beliefs. He calls these powers or energies by their ancient names, eros, mars, the muses, mammon, and dominion (worldview, comprehensive moral vision, religion). "Humans are sexual, political, economic, cultural, and religious creatures. Each one of these dimensions of life involves a certain

Theological ethics must attempt to answer the question: How do we organize the common life in a global era? He argues that the Christian metaphysical moral vision is best suited to do this job.

> I am persuaded that the Christian faith is the most valid worldview or metaphysical moral vision available to humanity, but I recognize that others have other views that we have to encounter and heed, and that we may gain from other faiths in a globalizing world.[24]

Finally, theological ethics must guide the emerging process toward the New Jerusalem. This is to say, influence and "channel the energy of this massive civilization shift called globalization so that it more nearly corresponds to the ultimately redemptive tides of history God intends, and not only to critique or resist it hopelessly."[25]

Critique of Stackhouse's Theologies of History and Globalization

There is plenty to quarrel about with Stackhouse's theologies of history and globalization, but my interest is not to plow the obvious ground or work over what others have done. We, therefore, need not bother repeating what many scholars disagree with:

(a) the privileged position he assigns to Christianity

(b) his identification of the central theological-ethical question

---

potentiality and needs an institutional matrix to house, guide and channel its energies." Stackhouse, "Introduction" in Stackhouse and Browning, *God and Globalization*, 2:5. In another place, he writes:
> [P]eople carve out spheres of social activity, clusters of institutions that house, guide, and constrain, and in certain ways, permit, even encourage, these powers to operate. Each sphere is regulated by customary or legislated rules, and each is defined by its own specification of ends and means, as these accord with the nature of the activity and its place in the whole society or culture. Each sphere develops methods of fulfilling its own standards, ways to mark accomplished goals, definitions of excellence, and standards of success. (See Stackhouse and Paris, *God and Globalization*, 1:39.)

24. Stackhouse, *God and Globalization*, 4:7. Stackhouse argues that the adoption of Christian religious values and Western cultural values by others will enable them to participate fully in the globalization process. This, he insists, is not a call for them to be Christians, but to understand and appropriate the values that have created globalization as a world process.

25. Ibid., 4:248.

(challenge) of the global age as the search for the religion that must form the center of the emerging global society[26]
(c) the validity of universal moral norms
(d) his metanarrative of the Christian faith
(e) his position that globalization is the work of God and not a destructive imperialism of the dominant economies
(f) his interpretation of non-Western cultures
(g) the significant place he gives to Kuyper's idea of sphere of sovereignty which was "misused" in apartheid South Africa.[27]

These are worthy issues with which to engage Stackhouse, but disagreement on them will not necessarily torpedo and sink his theoretical edifice. In my opinion, we need to set aside all these for now and focus on his theology of history, which appears as a remake of Hegel's theory of the dialectics of the civil society as stated in the *Philosophy of Right*. And this unintended (unstated) close connection with Hegel calls for a *Serequeberhanian-Heideggerian* "de-structive [de-structuring] reading"[28] of the theory of civil society that undergirds Stackhouse's theology of history.

---

26. Schweiker, "Public Theology," 123–38.

27. Except for the brief mention of spheres of life, we did not really explore this dimension of Stackhouse's thought. Many scholars have criticized him for his "undiscerning" appropriation of Abraham Kuyper's ideas. For example, see Paris, "African and African-American Understanding," 263–80.

28. This phrase is borrowed from Serequeberhan (*Contested Memory*, 28n87) who in turn borrowed it from Martin Heidegger. This is how Serequeberhan explains it:
> I borrowed the notion of "destruction" [*Destrucktion*] from Martin Heidegger's *Being and Time*, pt. 1, sec. 6 (New York: Harper & Row, 1962). In brief, such as a de-structive reading is a radical exegesis firmly implanted in the text that undermines the text from within and in terms of the central notions on which the text in question is grounded and in so doing reveals the hidden impulses articulated in the text. The hyphen in the variations of this term, which I utilize, is a short-hand for the explication that Heidegger gives of this term. It stresses that what is intended is not the "destruction"—i.e., the elimination, annihilation, or demolition—of what is in question, but rather its critical unpacking or opening up to a radical inquiry and interrogation. . . . As it is well know Heidegger utilized such a reading in order to pierce through the ontological tradition and uncover the "true" Greek source. Nostalgia for the Greeks is what directed his efforts. My efforts, on the other hand, are aimed at peeling away, from the icons of the occidental tradition, the veneer of being thinkers of human freedom that they have amassed within this tradition and in doing, to reveal the way this very veneer allows the conceptualization of the global dominance of the West—presented by them—to be seen as an effort aimed at the actuality of human freedom. (*Contested Memory*, 28n87.)

What calls for attention is not just the similarity between Hegel's theory of the civil society and Stackhouse's notion of social common space between the individual/family unit and the state, but, rather the hidden impulses of the a "space" globalizing itself, the dialectics of the complete realization of the principle of ecclesia.[29]

The impulses coagulate around an aporia or paradox in the Hegelian theory of civil society.[30] Western expansion and globalization is the exportation and globalization of this aporia. It is clear from Hegel's exposition of the civil society that poverty ("propertyless will") is an inevitable outcome of the workings of civil society; poverty is a norm rooted and sustained in the normal, healthy socioeconomic dynamic of civil society.[31] For Hegel the "excess wealth" created by modern civil society is only the flipside of its "excess poverty" and thus the abolition of poverty is the central challenge of modern society.[32] Hegel advised that in order to solve this problem—that is, "resolve" the aporia in the theory—the European civil society has to be exported; foreign lands must be colonized.[33] The need to export or expand outside the geographic base of Europe does not arise out of some accident, it is the very "inner dialectic of civil society."[34] The exportation of poverty does not really resolve the aporia, "rather, it simply displaces and duplicates, or reinvents, the paradox of civil society on a new soil. . . . This whole development is viewed by Hegel as the spread of culture and civilization."[35]

I am not sure if Stackhouse is fully aware of this shadow side of Hegel's theory of the civil society which informed his thinking as mediated by Kuyper's theory of sovereign spheres. In any case, what is important is that

---

29. The analysis below is indebted to Serequeberhan, *Contested Memory*, 63–106.

30. Stackhouse alludes to some new, contemporary theories of civil society in his 2009 presidential address to the American Theological Society. (See Stackhouse, "Framing the Global Ethos," 8.) While these theories can shed some light on his understanding of creative democracy and social theory of politics, they cannot carry the weight of his philosophy of history. They do not have the dialectics to shed light on the progress of history, of the dynamics of ecclesia. Stackhouse's theory of the ecclesia, which we have explained so far, is in a certain sense a cross between what he calls "contemporary and older views" of civil society. So it is not out of place here to focus on part of the "combo" that elucidates on the dialectics of history since the focus of this essay is on his theology of history.

31. Hegel, *Philosophy of Right*, 189–200.

32. Ibid., par. 245 and addition to par. 244.

33. Ibid., pars. 240–49.

34. Ibid., par. 246.

35. Serequeberhan, *Contested Memory*, 83–84.

Stackhouse is deafeningly silent on the law of motion that propels the idea of common space from its humble beginnings in western Europe to the universal New Jerusalem. Maybe, he is not really silent: by latching on to capitalism and corporation (*worldly ecclesia*) he presumed or presupposed the working of the inner dialectic of the civil society. He then assumed that by and large capitalism delivers more prosperity than poverty. His usual response to this query about poverty runs like this: "The new ethos that is being formed is pulling millions out of poverty while the young see hope in the new development—even if very large numbers of people are still caught in economic and cultural stagnation."[36] This is at best only a "resolution" of the aporia from *without* the theory that he relies upon to undergird his theology.

Stackhouse can resolve the paradox of the Hegelian theory of civil society by arguing that Hegel got himself into the quagmire by attaching the *will* to property. The solution is to divorce the two in the theory. Alas, this route is blocked for Stackhouse by his sturdy support for private property, the free market system, and capitalism. The real easy option for him to take is to redefine or expand the central theological challenge of the global age to include poverty reduction or abolition. The unforgiving dialectics of civil society that is the law of motion of history, the journey to ultimate destiny of New Jerusalem neither grants him nor any democratic ethical life much choice. Or, does it?

In any case, if we can neither blame Stackhouse for the shadow side of the theory of civil society nor castigate him for the dream of an urban cosmopolitan New Jerusalem then we can at least ask of him this: Why is poverty reduction or abolition not the central theological challenge of the global age given that poverty rides (not on donkey's back but on a jet plane) the civil society highway to the holy New Jerusalem? Why make the search for the religious core of the emerging global society the number one theological and ethical issue?

Concluding Remarks

Stackhouse is a prominent member of modern social ethics intelligentsia and many scholars regard him as an "establishment figure" in this court. This is not the best reading of his work or ethical thought. While he remains a key, widely respected thinker, he evades modern social ethics with

36. Stackhouse, "Framing the Global Ethos," 5.

its focus on moral and religious relativism, contextualization, particularizing predicates, disposition (virtue and habits), or liberation. His is about the movement of history toward a goal, the realization of the universal New Jerusalem, the expanded ecclesia. Neither the state or the race nor economic growth is the highest good. The actualization of the New Jerusalem stands above all of them. His focus was to work out the logic of history and from the logic of history derive an objectively valid value system, the standards to judge different religions and social systems. And theology is to tell us whether a specific religion, society, or tradition is at the core fundamentally true.

> Both the *theos* and *logos* of theology drive it toward cosmopolitan perspectives of a normative and universal sort. . . . [We have to encounter] the fact that we face a world of multiple religions and cultural traditions that cannot all be equally valid. At this level, to appeal to the power and significance of our religion in our context simply does not suffice. After all, the distinctive feature of religion is that it claims to have some insight about a real, other world that is manifest in or related to this one. And the distinctive claim of theology is that it can critically assess and evaluate those claims with the recognition that some of them may be valid even if many are false or even evil. If this is not possible, if theology cannot reach cross-culturally, cross-historically, cross-religiously, and finally transcendentally, even religion loses sight of the character and content of its "more," and sinks into the collective consciousness of what is going on in this or that social history, serving only the totemic flag of all those mundane interests which preoccupy the world without God.[37]

From here Stackhouse assigns the historical problem of understanding globalization to ethics; precisely, to theological ethics that can craft the system of values and religious symbols to guide its proper functioning. The history and ethics of globalization are in one sense about how the experience of the emerging global society is both shaped and evaluated. He is driven to bring philosophy of history and ethics closer together. Ethics, he believes, must be situated or undergirded by the theological contemplation of the panorama of history. His philosophy of history provides the systematic orientation to ethics in general and to special studies on select subject matters.

---

37. Stackhouse, "Social Theory," 37–38.

CHAPTER FOUR

Emergence and "Science of Ethos": Toward a Tillichian Ethical Framework

Opening Word

THE SECOND PHASE OF our ethical methodology as laid out in chapter 1 involves relating the analysis of social problems to a theological or philosophical framework so as to relate their framing and the search for their solution to a faith tradition or worldview. The effort to show this connection often requires complex cultural, theological, and philosophical analyses. First, the ethicist must start with an idea of what the community considers as its ultimate point of reference, ultimate mystery, ultimate reality, the ultimate concern, the Unconditional, God. Second, she must show how the creative cultural-moral functions (the symbolic order of meaning and purpose) of human life in that community or faith tradition are oriented to this reference (ground of being or context) to provide meaning and fulfillment for personal and social existence. Finally, she is hoping that this construction and reconstruction provide an orientation for human beings in the world. Such a construction is always a vision of human's place in the world and what can facilitate the flourishing of human life.

In this chapter we will engage with the thought of Paul Tillich, supplemented by that of Gordon Kaufman, as seen through the biology of emergence. The discussions show how multiple discipline can be combined to construct or reconstruct a philosophical framework, and how this effort can profoundly affect one's understanding of the ethical task itself. Thus, this chapter not only sheds light on the labor required to properly fashion the second stage of our methodology as laid out in chapter 1, but it also shows the working of Tillich's ethical methodology.

Above all, the philosophical discussions on emergence and ethics give us insight on how to develop an ethical (symbolic) framework or a

Emergence and "Science of Ethos": Toward a Tillichian Ethical Framework

methodology of constructive theological-ethics. They also prepare the student in the art of imaginative construction of a comprehensive and coherent picture of ethics of community or society.

Chapter Introduction

This chapter offers an ethical framework informed by *emergence*. In a religious interpretation, emergence has recently been characterized as the underlying creative principle of nature or "the divine." In order to sketch out the contours of this framework, we combined two streams of thought: one is based on the current effort to work out the implications of emergence, nature's mode of creativity; the other is about conceptualizing ethics as humans' attempt to align with their ground of being. Theologian Gordon Kaufman[1] and biologist Stuart Kauffman[2] are some of the scholars who have turned to interpreting the natural phenomenon of emergence in religious terms. Paul Tillich[3] conceptualized ethics (which he called "science of ethos," "science of culture") as the reach of human sociality toward and expressing "the Unconditional." For him, the concern of ethics is about the creative functions of human life; tracing and clarifying the lure of mystery at work in culturally-creative actions of persons and social groups.

If we go the way of emergentist-philosophers who are gesturing us to see emergence as a form of creativity, the unconditional, non-predetermined creative impulse, then the task of ethics is to show how cultural-moral institutions of civilizations can express this underlying reality. At least, this is one veritable way to explore the connections between emergence and ethics. This vista provides a doorway for ethicists to examine the implications of emergence as a philosophical position for ethical thinking and analysis. Ethics here has the meaning of a theory of culture, customs and mores (*Sittlichkeit*) and not that of demand and duty (*Moralität*).

The ethical framework I am developing here does not require us to make a commitment to the idea of creativity as God or God as creativity. One may either believe that behind the creative process which fosters emergence there is no particular existent being (as both Gordon Kaufman and Stuart Kauffman do) or believe that emergence is the process God uses to maintain on-going creativity as it courses toward higher levels of

1. Kaufman, *In the Beginning . . . Creativity*; Kaufman, "Religious Interpretation," 915–28.
2. Kauffman, "Beyond Reductionism," 905, 913–14.
3. Tillich, *System of Sciences*; Tillich, *Systematic Theology, Vol. III*.

complexification. The issue raised and addressed here is how human creativity can reflect divine or *serendipitous creativity*—that is, how is cultural-moral dimension of human sociality in-formed, pre-formed, and formed by the power that sustains life, by the ground of existence. It is to ask the pertinent ethical question about emergence: what pattern of human sociality, modes of being, the unfolding of social being would indicate the necessary connection between human creativity and the "vast ceaseless creativity" in the universe; that is, what is the groundedness of human projects and work in the ultimate creativity which is in operation in the universe? Let me recast this thought. First it is posited (as we shall see below) that divine (serendipitous) creativity is widening and deepening human historical existence and human lives are caught in this trajectory-context. Then the question becomes: how can (do) culturally creative-moral projects and activities fittingly and responsibly feel "at home" in it?

It is pertinent at this juncture to offer a brief description of emergence as it is used in this paper. By emergence I mean novel properties, traits that arise from a given set of matter in the right sort of organized complexity. The properties are novel not only because they cannot be found at lower levels of complexity, but are also unpredictable phenomena produced by the interactions between preexisting elements or parts. The operation of the novel (higher) forms (properties, causal capacities or systems) is often not reducible to the preexisting or lower parts. Emergence names the process whereby "the "underivable" can be birthed amid many derivable conditions.[4]

Emergence is a phenomenon that takes place when any of these processes or some combination of them occurs: bottom-up and top-down causal interactivity, supervenience, self-organization, and autopoiesis.[5] In a world where every system is potentially opened to move to "location" other than where it is now in the "possibility space," these processes do work to bring new and unpredictable phenomena in nature. With this kind of possibilities and contingency, no one person can know all future actualities. In emergentist thinking the world is experimental, unfinished; it is in process and is a process. The fact that complexity can arise from simple elements simply calls our attention to this: every set of relations or systems is a being which is not yet "given," only a *transcendere*.

---

4. Tillich, *Systematic Theology*, 3:324.
5. Gregersen, "Emergence and Complexity," 767–83; Ellis, "Physics, Complexity," 752–66.

This understanding of emergence rides on two core ideas in the contemporary discussions of emergency: *contingency* and *possibilities*.[6] The phenomenon of emergency presents us with pure possibilities—the *novum* is always becoming. Emergence carries with it the notion that in every combination of elements there is a *not-yet* which names "both a surplus and a remainder over what-has-become."[7] This promise or gift of becoming is at the cost of contingency. The animating power or thrust of emergence "dwells in the region of the not-yet, a place where entrance and, above all, final content are marked by an enduring indeterminacy."[8]

As a notion of philosophy, emergence also expresses an ethos, an orientation to existential relationships and the existentially meaningful in the here and now. For instance, the spirit or spiritual *presence* in emergentist thinking is not a transcendental phenomenon, perched on some supernatural plane as against the world of moral-cultural situations. It is not opposed to finite historicality. It is immanent to all finite life and inseparable from it. The spirit as an emergent self, the underivably new, though is beyond and more than the mere physical (natural, human, and cultural—life) it is with and within (and not above) the structures and dynamics of complex nature and culture.

In general, theologians who have worked on emergence have approached it as an explanatory framework against physicalism (ontological reductionism) and God/spirit and nature/material-world dualism in the interpretation of the world. It is also used to "map an understanding of divine action, yet without making God's action secondary in relation to the base of the material world."[9] Emergence can also offer us a paradigm to think about social relations if it is turned into a series of ethical arguments. Emergence is a uniquely suited paradigm to address the uncertainties of modern social life in an open, globalizing world, to inform an ethical theory of adaptation to complexity, and to help us investigate how human creativity can be nudged to reflect its underlying ontological creativity. The starting point for turning the philosophy of emergence into a series of ethical arguments is to note the aspects of philosophical understanding of emergence that could inform ethical theories. Three of these aspects readily come to mind. First, the philosophical understanding of emergence posits

---

6. Van Huyssteen, *Alone in the World?*; Gregersen, "Emergence and Complexity," 767–69.

7. Anderson, "Transcending Without Transcendence," 696.

8. Bloch, *Literary Essays*, 69.

9. Gregersen, "Emergence and Complexity," 781.

that systems are hugely *unpredictable*. What could be more unpredictable than mental properties emerging from a natural world? So at the core of one of emergentist philosophers' definition of the subject matter is unpredictability. Philip Clayton, a leading emergentist philosopher, maintains that "emergence is the view that new and unpredictable phenomenon are naturally produced by interactions in nature; that these new structures, organisms, and ideas are not reducible to the subsystems on which they depend, and that the newly evolved realities in turn exercise a causal influence on the parts out of which they arose."[10] Second, emergence, understood as a philosophical position, questions the whole method of explaining events or phenomena in terms of initial conditions, constituent parts, and underlying laws. The import of this is that emergence holds a crucial key to understanding creativity, the adaptive process of social systems, and capacity of human socialities for self-complexification. Third, showing how the cultural-creative actions of communities can express the underlying non-predetermined creative impulse of all existence.

The above representation of the contemporary discourse on emergence is far from being comprehensive. I have provided this thumbnail sketch of the theory of emergence as a way of priming the reader for Kaufman's religious interpretation of emergence and Tillich's concept of *kairos* and "the underivable new." Kaufman conceptualizes God as "the ongoing creativity in the world" "instead of as The Creator."[11] For Kaufman creativity, is not limited to the originative processes of the Big Bang and evolution, but includes human symbolic creativity. He then proceeded to argue that emergence is another word for creativity:

> [E]mergence... has come to be increasingly used in some sciences and philosophy to characterize evolutionary developments in which new realities, not reducible to previous stages of evolution, have appeared. In our Western cultures and religions, we also have, of course, a very old word for coming into being, or the bringing into being, of significant realities that had not previously existed: creation.[12]

We are getting ahead of ourselves. Let me now indicate how we intend to proceed with the development of this chapter. In section one, I will lay out the religious interpretation of emergence. Here I will specifically focus

10. Clayton, *Minds and Emergence*, vi.
11. Kauffman, "Beyond Reductionism," 915.
12. Ibid., 915–16.

on the work of theologian Gordon Kaufman who over many years have been developing this interpretation.[13] The next section will lay out Tillich's idea of ethics as ethos. I have turned to Tillich for two reasons. First, for him ethics is about how to orient the cultural functions of human life to the underlying principle of ontological dynamic creativity, the ground of being, the Unconditional. The systematic character of Tillich's "science of ethos" makes it easy to craft a framework with which to explore the nature of ethics as informed by emergence. Second, Kaufman's notion of ethics, as we shall discover, appears to be also focused on orienting the creative-cultural functions of human life toward the "serendipitous creativity."

In turning to Kaufman and Tillich I am aware and cautious of the fact that there are differences in their metaphysical pictures of the world. Tillich paints the picture of "ground of being" or "being-itself" and Kaufman has that of "dynamic creativity," or "mystery." Kaufman himself pointed this out in his 2001 essay in the journal *Zygon*.[14] The two different theological pictures should lead to different ways of doing ethics. I have tried to avoid apparent conflict by putting the accent on Tillich's metaphysical ideas—as argued below, Kaufman's religious interpretation of emergence has moved the notion from just being a scientific hypothesis or an explanatory framework to a metaphysical proposition. Besides, the way I am using Tillich's notion of ethics—that of "science of ethos"— enables me to fruitfully combine the insights of Kaufman's theologization of emergence with Tillich's methodology of theological-ethics to construct a creativity-oriented ethical framework. I understand Tillich to be arguing that ethical reasoning should attempt to orient forms of human sociality toward the ultimate point of reference in a given community. So once Kaufman, as we shall see, elevated emergence (serendipitous creativity) as a possible point of ultimate reference it prompted an ethicist comfortable with the Tillichian approach to explore how human cultural institutions should be oriented to it.

Section three actually develops such a framework. It is shown that such a framework will facilitate the realization of distinctively human potentialities, flourishing, and fulfillment. Summary and concluding remarks follow.

---

13. Kaufman, *In Face of Mystery*; Kaufman, *In the Beginning*; Kaufman, "Religious Interpretation."
14. Kaufman, "Re-conceiving God and Humanity," 335–48.

Section One: Kaufman's Creative Interpretation of Emergence

Kaufman thinks of God as *serendipitous creativity* (instead of agential Creator).[15] The vast, magnificent panorama of creativity and dynamism that through time brings new modes of reality into being is interpreted as clue or key to the ultimate reality. More precisely, he defines serendipitous creativity

> as a notion that can be used to describe and interpret the enormous expansion and complexification of the physical universe from *the Big Bang onward,* as well as the *evolution of life here on Earth* and the gradual emergence of *human historical existence.* This whole vast cosmic process... has frequently produced much more than would have been expected or seemed possible, given previously prevailing circumstances.[16]

From the definition above, we can note three forms or modalities of creativity that inform Kaufman's notion of serendipitous creativity. There is what he calls creativity1 that ushered in the beginning of the universe through the Big Bang. The second modality (creativity2) is the ongoing complexification of realities in the course of biological evolution that has brought into being innumerable quantity of creatures, including humans. The third mode is called *symbolic creativity* or creativity3, which has brought into being novel forms of organizations and extraordinary complex cultures. This form is about human sociality in its historical creativity and dynamism.[17]

Kaufman argues that the creativity he has described is not a force, a cause, not a personal agential being, and "not a quasi scientific explanation of why and how new realities come into being."[18] It is a word used to identify and call attention to the mysteries that pertain to the Big Bang, biological evolution of life, and human sociocultural life plus the further meaning of "coming into being of the new." "The concept of creativity in no way explains how or why new realities have come into being; rather it simply

---

15. Kaufman, *In Face of Mystery*; Kaufman, *In the Beginning*; Kaufman, *Jesus and Creativity*; Kaufman, "Religious Interpretation."

16. Kaufman, *In the Beginning,* 43; italics added.

17. Kaufman, "Religious Interpretation," 915–16; Kaufman, *In the Beginning,* 76, 84–85, 100.

18. Kaufman, *In the Beginning,* 71; Kaufman, "Religious Interpretation," 927.

Emergence and "Science of Ethos": Toward a Tillichian Ethical Framework

gives a name to the profoundly mysterious fact that novel realities have come into existence in the course of time."[19] This creativity, he equates with *emergence*, believing that anywhere we see creativity or believe that it has occurred a new emergence has happened.[20] He then states that anywhere we find creativity, emergence, there is always "profound mystery." Once he lined up "coming into being of the new," creativity, dynamic emergence, and mystery, he makes the bold move to give it a religious name.[21]

> I suggest that instead of taking it for granted that "God" is the name of a creator-person who has brought everything into being, we will find it illuminating to think of God as the religious name for the profound mystery of creativity—the mystery of emergence, in and through evolutionary and other originative processes, of novelty in the world.[22]

He chose to do this; that is name God as creativity or creativity as God, because he thought creativity was the defining mark of God in the Abrahamic traditions.[23]

As I have stated before one does not necessarily have to agree with Kaufman that God is creativity and creativity is God to explore the vista for ethical thinking that his naming or renaming of emergence opens up. For me, his religious interpretation of emergence throws up four significant ideas for exploring the intersection of emergentist philosophy and theological-ethics. First, creativity (and hence emergence) is not formless. Creativity, emergence, is not only the mystery, potentiality, and the new, but it also mediates all that happens in the universe. Although, Kaufman does not explicitly state the form-nature of his creativity, it is obvious that it is not a perpetually chaotic power. It is self-organizing. It is the depth dimension, the source and unity of being, form, and articulation. There are, nonetheless, fleeting references to form-character of the "overflowing fountain of creativity" which gives particular structure and orderliness to things. This striving for form, which he calls "directional movements" in the cosmic process, is working in and through all things to increasingly manifest complex forms of order.

19. Kaufman, *In the Beginning*, 71.
20. Kaufman, "Religious Interpretation," 925.
21. Ibid., 927; Kaufman, *In the Beginning*, 73.
22. Kaufman, "Religious Interpretation," 916.
23. Ibid., 926.

This brings us to the second point. According to Kaufman, one of the trajectories of the cosmic movements is toward "the authentically human and humane," which is "pressing toward our further humanization, encouraging the establishment and strengthening of communities of love and peace and justice in an ecologically sustainable world."[24] It is important to pause here in order to note that Kaufman has made attempts to move away from this kind of teleological suggestions in his more recent works.[25] In a personal email to me on January 7, 2008 he disavows the idea that there is a pressing toward increasing humanization. On my part, I think that emergence as nature's mode of creativity is not entirely inimical to all suggestions of teleology—at least at the symbolic level. Emergence as a natural process may be blind, but we as humans cannot take as normative existential despair, meaninglessness, as the core of our togetherness. We do guide natural process of creativity, in the mode Kaufman himself regards as bio-historical, to trajectory we think might benefit us. This movement of creativity at the level sufficiently grasped by humans needs some determinate ends in terms of which its results can be meaningfully assessed on the biohistorical plane. Men and women are inclined to make sense of the infinitude that embeds and surpasses the limits of their finite existence.

Those who completely reject any association of telos with emergence, perhaps, have not grasped some of the crucial dimensions of emergence as nature's mode of creativity. Creativity is both finite and infinite, suspended between being and nonbeing. It is infinite because it is not intrinsically related to the any determinate order of things. It has no goal or telos and does not proceed according to any pre-given end. In relating to itself without meaning, it engages its nonbeingness, its indeterminate and indeterminable possibility. In its being-in-the world it has to have being, limit, and determination. This is the Kierkegaardian tragic bind of emergence in relating itself to itself. There is a basic inability to be or not to be. It is both *be* and *not be* anything determinable. On its "be" aspect, its being-in-the-world, we humans attempt to discern or affix some "telos" if we are to proceed with the business of ordering our forms of sociality.

This insight brings us to another crucial point. Emergence as conceptualized, at least by one interpretation, allows for downward causation. In this sense, the concept accommodates true chance or indeterminacy, and

---

24. Kaufman, *In Face of Mystery*, 296, 370; see also 339, 397.

25. Kaufman, *In the Beginning*; Kaufman, *Jesus and Creativity*; Kaufman, "Religious Interpretation."

events at lower realms of space and time are subject to selection pressure from formal autocatalytic configurations above.[26] We know that emergence, creativity, has brought forth teleologically oriented human beings.[27] Their actions can impact some directionality, though not full-blown teleology to the dynamics, propensities of serendipitous creativity. Those aspects of creativity that are in catalytic communication with human teleology will tend to reinforce each other. Thus, there may be some drive toward more organization, "ascendancy" to use the word of ecologist Ulanowicz. He maintains that there are two processes at work in creativity:

> The deeper view of nature that process ecology reveals is one of a nearly balanced agonism between two tendencies. One propensity is the drift of the second law towards the dead and disordered that has precipitated a "cosmology of despair" so fashionable among academics. Its opposite is the drive towards ever more organized and coherent configurations of processes, such as earmark the presence of life. The virtual parity of these agonists in the framework of process ecology lends intellectual license to those who would choose to entertain a universal "cosmology of hope."[28]

Borrowing the insights of Ulanowicz on ecological development, we can say that the combined effect of autocatalyticism and directionality may serve to increase the humanization tendency of creativity.[29] Put differently, those dynamics of serendipitous creativity that most effectively participate in humanization becomes dominant over time. Under the influence of civilization, symbolic creativity by biohistorical beings increases—they produce an increasing amount of output (good or bad ideas, practices, and processes) on how best to organize human coexistence. The outputs are not completely free floating agents able to do whatever they can in the system. As civilization moves forward there are also increasing constraints (such as certain social practices, agencies) that appear in the evolutionary process to guide the flow and development of the output and in this way help to contribute to the humanization process. At times these constraints work well to channel the output with the greatest potentials for humanization forward and at other times they fail. Civilization at its best is a process that attempts

---

26. Ulanowicz, "Ecology, a Dialog," 34–52.
27. Rue, "Emergence," 829–935.
28. Ulanowicz, "Ecosystem Dynamics," 249.
29. Ulanowicz, "Ecology, a Dialog"; Ulanowicz, "Ecosystem Dynamics"; Ulanowicz, "Emergence, Naturally!," 945–50.

to maximally constraint the distribution of ideas, practices, and processes to flow in certain direction and contribute to the autocatalysis itself. All this does not imply a linear sense of smooth progress. For civilization also embeds within itself certain "overheads" that counter this tendency. The overheads, as Ulanowicz sees them are redundancies, discarded, irrelevant ideas, processes and practices, and "evils" of a system that do create gaps, disruptions in its armor which in periods of stress or crisis are capable of allowing the system to adapt and creatively advance.[30] On the whole, the validity of the ethical framework developed in this chapter does not really depend on a commitment to telos in creativity. All it posits is that humans who do organize their forms of sociality with purposes in mind are well served if they orient their meaning-seeking projects to their understanding of ultimate reality. And thus append a telic dimension to the creativity.

Let us now turn to the third of the four significant ideas thrown up by Kaufman's religious interpretation of emergence. He identifies creativity as a sort of source of being for human historical existence. Creativity$_3$ emerged from and is undergirded by creativity$_1$ and creativity$_2$. Finally, there is the idea of human beings as *biohistorical* beings. Human development is shaped by both biological evolution and historical development. They are a resultant of natural biological processes and historico-cultural processes. These two processes are not fundamentally different, but as noted earlier, rather different modalities of creativity that continue to manifest its deep mystery. Human historical existence, that is the increasingly complex sociocultural forms of life are powered by serendipitously engendered auto-catalytic historical process.[31] In a certain sense, the dynamics of human history is God's participation in history.

The four ideas suggest that human creativity is a form of participation in creativity. Then the task of ethics, as we will soon learn from Tillich, is to develop the ideational framework and cultural-moral institutions that reflect the creative ground. It is in this trajectory of thought that I intend to explore the connections between emergence and ethics. Bringing this particular Tillichian concept of ethics to bear upon the emergence and emergentist philosophy and theology as crafted by Kaufman is not like mixing oil and water. There is something in Kaufman's thinking as he develops his interpretation of emergence as creativity that invites notion of ethics as fundamental orientation to the context and ground of being, the

30. Ulanowicz, "Ecology, a Dialog," 248.
31. Kaufman, *In the Beginning*, 99.

Emergence and "Science of Ethos": Toward a Tillichian Ethical Framework

ultimate creativity. First, for him God (and, in his interpretation, creativity) is the ultimate point of reference in terms of which all human life is to be understood and judged—human lives are to be fundamentally oriented to this point of reference.[32] Second, even beyond serving as "pull factor," serendipitous or hidden creativity is nudging human existence into fuller humanity and humaneness; the trajectory of cosmic and historical forces "is pressing us toward a more humane world," that is, the deepening and widening of human coexistence.[33]

Third, his religious interpretation of emergence has moved the concept from just being a scientific hypothesis or theorem to a metaphysical proposition. Emergence is a phenomenon that cannot be thingified; it is creativity that cannot be conditioned. Creativity as God, God as creativity, is an *eros* (my characterization) that is with and within biohistorical existence but it is beyond and more than any historicality. It is a profound mystery of the unconditional. It expresses an orientation, a directional movement, the pursuit of "coming into being of the new." Kaufman is putting forward to us a metaphysical proposition about "Why is there Something and no Nothing?" Agreed, it is heavily informed by modern science, it is nonetheless metaphysics. As Tillich puts it, "every proposition of a creative metaphysics is an expression of an ethos; every ethos expresses a metaphysics. This is why a metaphysician like Spinoza called his metaphysics *Ethics*."[34]

Fourth, Kaufman's religious interpretation of emergence invites Tillichian approach to ethics because of what he explicitly stated about the implication of his concepts of *serendipitous creativity* and *biohistorical beings*. He wrote:

> If God is understood now as the creativity manifest throughout the cosmos, and we humans [biohistorical beings] are understood as deeply embedded in, and basically sustained by, the web of life on planet Earth, then our attitudes and activities are to be ordered in terms of (a) what fits properly into the web of living creativity, all members of which are neighbors that we should love, and (b) what is in response to, and further contributes to, the ongoing creative development of our trajectory (the activity of God) within this web.[35]

---

32. Kaufman, *In Face of Mystery*; Kaufman, *In the Beginning*, 40.
33. Kaufman, *In the Beginning*, 125, 51, 61–62, 105–6.
34. Tillich, *System of Sciences*, 201.
35. Kaufman, *In the Beginning*, 125–26.

Methods of Ethical Analysis

Before we proceed to Tillich's idea of ethics, it is important to mention that the orientation of ethics to the ground and context of human life will not necessarily allow us to derive norms for concrete cases.[36] This is particularly so for Kaufman's religious interpretation of emergence or creativity. Not only that there are no directing principles derivable from the concept of random creativity, but also it suggests no moral imperative. Though creativity proceeds by taking forms to real-ize (making things real to our observation) beings there is no obligation of potentiality to become actuality. Tillich, on the other hand, believes that humans have the obligation to actualize their potentialities, their true being to become their actual being.[37] There is no such obligation in Kaufman's thinking because the ultimate belongingness of biological evolution that produced humans and the symbolic creativity that turns them into biohistorical beings were never separated. There is no estrangement and there is no particular distinction between existence and essence as we find in Tillich's thought.

Section Two: Tillich Concept of Ethics

Human beings participate in creativity not only because they are situated in it, but also because they change what they receive to create new products of culture and in the process transform themselves. In the hands of humans the dynamics of creativity is combined with meaningful structure. Humans are both products and bearers of creativity. Thus, in their bio-historical existence, the creation of self-transforming and self-transcending acts, activity, and artifacts, they are driven by life's inner dynamics.

Tillich considers culture to be the creation of a "universe of meaning" and this creation is only the fulfillment of the universe of being, the working out of the potentialities and possibilities of the creative dynamics. In each culture or group creativity is given its particularity and expressive ability by the form through which it is shown forth.[38] According to Tillich, there are three elements in all cultural creativity: subject matter, form, and substance. *Subject matter*: in every culture certain objects of all that is available is chosen as significant in the universe of means and ends or in the universe of expression. The *form* makes the cultural creation what it is. *Substance*: the encounter of every group or culture with the underlying reality

---

36. Ibid., 63.
37. Tillich, *Morality and Beyond*, 20–24.
38. Tillich, *Systematic Theology*, 3:84–85.

of serendipitous creativity (to use Kaufman's word) differs from encounter in another culture or place, "and this encounter in its totality and its depth is the substance" of a cultural creation.

> Whereas its subject matter is chosen and its form intended, its substance is, so to speak, the soil out of which it grows. Substance cannot be intended. It is unconsciously present in a culture, a group, an individual, giving passion and driving power to him [sic] who creates and the significance and power of meaning to his creations.[39]

Based on this close connection between culture and religion, Tillich once wrote "religion is the substance of culture, and culture is the form of religion." Culture is the form in which the basic concerns of religion expresses itself and religion gives meaning to culture.[40] Human historical existence is the form of creativity and creativity is the substance of culture, to reword the popular Tillich's statement in the light of our emphasis on the biohistorical plane of serendipitous creativity. If this idea is refracted through Kaufman's concept of biohistorical beings and creativity3 it means there is a two-way connection between serendipitous creativity and culture. On the one hand, human historicity expresses the creative ground and context of human lives and flourishing, and on the other it is the modality in which serendipitous creativity makes itself known in human experience. There are aspects or dimension of creativity that cannot express itself without historicity and human coexistence needs the source of creative depth and unconditioned dynamism. The basic Tillichian insight works against the establishment of dualism between religion and culture or in our case between culture and creativity.

Having said this we need to quickly add that the linkage between "form and substance" in human coexistence, according to Tillich, is not always intact. The nature of the ongoing connection is discernible in three forms: *theonomy, autonomy,* and *heteronomy*. When the creatural creations express the ultimacy of meaning, when they are directed toward the ultimate in being and meaning, he named it *theonomy*. When finite creativity, that is cultural expressions, fittingly and responsibly reflect underlying divine creativity it is tagged as *theonomous*. In a different language, it means the aim of cultural creations grasped by the *theos* is "initiation" into the profound mystery of creativity. But when human cultural creative projects

---

39. Ibid., 60.
40. Tillich, *Theology of Culture*, 42.

are independent (in terms of its orientation) from the underlying infinite creativity it is *autonomous*. Here it appears cultural expressions have lost (abandoned) their substance. It relies only on internal dynamics of historical life. Serendipitous creativity is always present, but the experience of its power of the *novum*, the "underivable new" is not. It is *heteronomous* (*heteros nomous*, outside, strange law) when the requirement to fittingly respond is imposed upon the creators of culture—submission of culture under ecclesiastic (political or what is considered divine) laws and this destroys or suppresses its inner dynamism.[41] Autonomy is sacrificed in the name of a principle that does not imply ultimacy and universality. There is a quest to intentionally (forcefully) direct autonomous creative activities to follow the norms of a deity, nationalistic state or group that is considered "sacred." In spite of the direction each of them may take under the circumstances it operates, Tillich is careful to note that neither heteronomy nor autonomy is totally estranged, "essentially separated" from the creative ground or context. Hence they each, together with theonomy, represent movement toward the ultimate point of reference, albeit at different degrees. But this movement is never fully realized. It is at best attained fragmentarily, but it is still a movement, an orientation by which the creative-cultural functions of human life become existentially meaningful.

We have been considering Tillich's idea of the connection between culture and its underlying dynamic ontological creativity. This is a necessary precursor to understanding his notion of ethics. Tillich thought of ethics not so much as discerning right and wrong, good and evil or even the virtues of persons that sustain a flourishing polity as an orientation of the cultural functions of human life to the ground of being, the ultimate concern, the ultimate point of reference, a non-anthropomorphic God. His "ethics" was his theology of culture, his theory of culture, "the science of ethos."

> Ethics is concerned with neither the good nor obligation [duty], with neither the personal order nor the legal order. It is not moral philosophy; it is the science of ethos, that is, the science of the realization of the Unconditional within meaning-fulfilling existential relationships.[42]

The emphasis on ethos as the subject matter of ethics invites us to think about how human creativity can orient itself to the Creativity that pervades,

---

41. Tillich, *Systematic Theology*, 3:249–52.
42. Tillich, *System of Sciences*, 203.

encompasses, and transcends it. How can we discern the meaning-giving traces of the Unconditional that is not lodged in some supernatural plane but is with and within the human cultural and natural structures and dynamics of existence? In simple terms, one is seeking to articulate the creative powers of cultural-moral situations as a depth dimension, expressing the "presence" intrinsic to it and pointing out how it can aspire to come to full alignment with Creativity. It may seem foolish to suggest that symbolic creativity (creativity3), which is a modality of Creativity, is out of line with it. It is here we need to come to back to Kaufman who defines for us what is the proper, acceptable thrust, directionality of human creativity in the cultural realm that broadens and deepens Creativity as it courses through bio-historical existence. This is to say, as he puts, that human creativity should be directed to be serving rather than restricting or countering "the forward movement into the open future on planet Earth of the cosmic serendipitous creativity to which we seek to be ultimately responsible."[43]

Kaufman is aware of the concern that introducing the language of acceptable qualifications in the phenomenon of emergence is problematic and may be even be troubling to some of the scientists and philosophers advocating the paradigm of emergence in scientific discourse. So he asks: "how can qualifications of this sort be reconciled with the claim that cosmic serendipitous creativity should be regarded as the ultimate point of reference in terms of which human existence is to be oriented, ordered, and normed?"[44] The explication of the answer is the task of the next section.

Section Three: Serendipitous Creativity and Ktizonomous Ethics

> In particular, I have argued that our sense of what we are doing in the world—of the meaningfulness of life and our concerns and projects—is transformed in important ways and immeasurably deepened if we are able to see these matters as significantly grounded in the serendipitous creativity at work in all things.... How best do we fit our own projects and activities into that wider and more fundamental movement?[45]

---

43. Kaufman, *In the Beginning*, 62.
44. Ibid., 61.
45. Kaufman, *In Face of Mystery*, 358.

Methods of Ethical Analysis

In his most recent book, *Jesus and Creativity* (2006), Kaufman pondered, albeit fleetingly, the ethical implication of his conception of God as simply the profound mystery of creativity. He reasoned that insofar our human actions draw from creativity3 it is possible to make claims about the relationship of such actions to the ultimate mystery of creativity. He then states that such a union with God (creativity) is not as important as exploring the "question about which trajectory (trajectories) in the universe [brought into place by Creativity, especially creativity1,] we should seek to be one with in our journey on planet Earth today."[46] Kaufman is not against seeing ethics as tracing and clarifying orientation to the Unconditional, the profound mystery. He is only, here, saying that it is better to orient to a trajectory of creativity, rather than to the whole wider creativity *per se*. We need not debate this narrowing of focus. It is better to explore what Kaufman thinks constitutes the model and criterion of such a trajectory. Without such "contents" his conception of God will be considered too vague and general to elicit orientation to the profound mystery, the Unconditional.

Fortunately, the "contents" are generated by his notion of *humaneness* or historicity. By humaneness, Kaufman is gesturing toward increasing complexity of sociocultural worlds marked by increasing interconnectedness, relationality. It is the whole complex of interrelating cultural functions that relate to meaning-fulfilling existential relationships "emphasizing the creation and sustenance of communities of love and freedom, reconciliation and peace," healing and inclusiveness in the quest for union with God, creativity.[47] The communities of love widen as they spread to all spheres of biohistorical order and are deepened in their orientation to creativity-trajectory.[48] In fact, he argues that the world in which humans live—the world pervaded by the mystery of creativity—is "a humane-seeking order (in certain significant respect, and we can give ourselves whole-heartedly to responsible life and work within it."[49]

Humaneness is a product of *productive creativity* and *destructive creativity*. Serendipitous creativity may not always manifest what is ultimately valuable to humans and thus it is the role of cultural institutions to provide some qualifications.

---

46. Kaufman, *Jesus and Creativity*, 26.
47. Ibid., 26.
48. Ibid., 71–72, 75.
49. Kaufman, *In Face of Mystery*, 339.

> Clearly creativity without qualification—creation of historical trajectories going in almost any direction—cannot be regarded as a norm appropriate or helpful for the guidance of human life and activity: our human creativity... must be directed toward bringing goods into the world, not evils, toward healing, toward resolving disputes through compromise and mediation, toward overcoming the destructive momentums... The human creation of trajectories of massive destructiveness must be put out of bounds.[50]

As stated above this sort of qualification goes against the grain of serendipitous creativity Kaufman has celebrated as God. Kaufman argues that though humans are a resultant of creativity they have evolved to bear responsibility over their actions, especially in the region of the cosmos affected by their actions and projects. Unlike the wider creativity in the universe, which can cause destruction of nature and human lives, humans cannot take as normative works of destructive creativity. What must be normative, he posits, must be "restricted to the *productive creativity* manifest on *planet Earth and its immediate environment*" (emphasis in the original). He added that:

> *productive creativity* alone is fitting, for clearly there is no reason to suppose that we humans have been in some way "authorized" (by an abstract cosmic creativity) to engage in extensive destruction of life and its ongoing momentums, which have taken thousands of millennia to emerge. Such a claim would manifest monstrous hubris and arrogance.[51]

In sum, we have discerned from Kaufman's and Tillich's ideas of ethics an accent on disciplined reflection on broadening and deepening of the horizons of embodied being in the orientation to the profound mystery of creativity (the unconditional) through out the realms of culture. Tillich called such an orientation, as we have learned, theonomy. It sets forth the idea of how human cultural creations are best related to the sacred, to symbol God (*theos*). As theologian Mark Lewis Taylor, a well-known interpreter of Tillich puts it "theonomy is being's desire, being pulled, or "grasped" as Tillich often put it, by the depth in autonomous life for which being hungers and toward which it moves, in spite of and through many forms of alienating and estranged existence."[52] This orientation is not im-

---

50. Kaufman, *In the Beginning*, 61.
51. Ibid., 61–62.
52. Taylor, *Religion, Politics*, 18.

Methods of Ethical Analysis

posed by an outside source; it is from the power of immanence operative within the functions of human history, within the biological, cultural, and social processes of human existence. Autonomy is only gifted with sacral normativity. Under the influence of theonomy, this inner dynamism of life deepens human world of moral-cultural functions and connects them to their depth, elicits an awareness of the profound mystery of creativity, the ultimate concern. It is important to note, as Taylor sums up the "donative" nature of the normativity of theonomy, that

> this unconditional is never forced upon culture, never imposed— it really cannot even be invited. Instead, it comes, it occurs, it is disclosed as a moral agent's or community's being grasped by its depth and so borne up and borne along, as it were, toward realization of its ideal norms, toward restoration of the unity of "the ought" with "the is."[53]

This way of characterizing theonomy is in tandem with Kaufman's idea of how creativity works in human historicity. Is this not his main point about characterizing creativity in the universe as serendipitous? Specifically, writing about the developments of symbolic creativity he stated that "these beginnings certainly could not have been the result of any deliberate human intentions and actions."[54]

In another place, he argued that history and historicity cannot be understood simply as a biological process. There is a striving toward *spirit*— "the symbolic order of meaning and purpose"— which is as important as the biological grounding.[55]

> Moreover, there is surely considerable justification for regarding this movement and striving (which we experience in ourselves and see in the humanity all around us) as having some significant relationship to "how things really are," as providing a clue, that is to say, to the ultimate mysteries with which we humans have to do.[56]

Along the same line of thought that led to the characterization of Tillich's ethics as *theonomous ethics*, we can call the form of ethics of creativity and emergence as so far set forth in our interpretation of Kaufman's theology as *ktizonomy* (the directedness and attraction of human cultural life

---

53. Taylor, "Paul Tillich's Ethics," 25.
54. Kaufman, *Jesus and Creativity*, 71.
55. Kaufman, *In Face of Mystery*, 257, 267.
56. Ibid., 267.

toward the creativity, *ktizo*; this is Greek for creativity). The immediate issue for those who consider creativity in its various modalities as providing the actual context for human lives and for which they are a part is *orientation*. According to Kaufman, orientation is about the reality "toward which our lives must in fact be oriented, if we are to be in effective rapport with the actual cosmic-historical movement in which we live."[57]

Based on the foregoing discussions on emergence and ethics, we can now develop an ethical (symbolic) framework or a methodology of constructive theological-ethics. The imaginative construction of a comprehensive and coherent picture of *ktizonomous* ethics involves these six dimensions. First, disciplined reflection on ethics (the variant known as the "science of ethos") must start with an idea of what it considers as the ultimate point of reference, ultimate mystery, ultimate reality, the ultimate concern, the Unconditional, God. "[I]t is important to recognize that if we choose to conclude that human life on its cultural and spiritual side has no metaphysical grounding, we are taking a long step toward seeing the world in nihilistic terms, that is, toward living with an underlying metaphysical despair about all human and humane values, hopes, and projects."[58] Second, show how this creative ground/context, ground of being operate to deepen and broaden being, complexify and interconnects what it has brought forth so that life, creation, is able to flourish; life grows and new forms emerge. It cannot be overemphasized that ethics is about the social, about facilitating "humaneness" so that human life can flourish and every person (always person-in-communion) can be all that he or she can be.

Third, the issue of ethics becomes how can the creative cultural-moral functions (the symbolic order of meaning and purpose) of human life be oriented to this ground of being or context to provide meaning and fulfillment for personal and social existence? The ultimate metaphysical-grounding-of-all-that-is may be taken as the creative ground, spirit, the ground of being, serendipitous creativity, dynamic ontological creativity, or substance—whatever is considered as the originative source of human beings, their earth and its immediate environment will do. Or, it is simply the anthropomorphic Father in heaven or God. This effort to show how the cultural-creative act should reflect God often involves complex cultural and philosophical analyses.

---

57. Ibid., 139; see also 330, 337–39, 358, 370–71; Kaufman, *Theological Method*, 64–67, 70–71.
58. Kaufman, *In Face of Mystery*, 268.

Methods of Ethical Analysis

The fourth dimension of the framework is showing how such reflection or approximation to the divine dynamic ontological creativity can be discerned. This involves defining some determinate ends that society desires besides creativity itself. Creativity itself requires them. The coursing of infinite creativity that overcomes resistance in order to create new forms and bring the new into being needs determinate ends in terms of which the products of its overcoming of resistance are meaningfully assessed on the biohistorical plane. The indicators include flourishing human life and deepening and widening of forms of human sociality. It may be argued that the directionality of the cosmic process which has brought forth human life and social development on earth "is drawing us onward toward a humane ordering of life—the coming of 'kingdom of God' in a 'new heaven and new earth,' as our religious traditions envisioned it."[59] In other words, it is moving toward a flourishing life of love, reconciliation, peace, justice, and inclusiveness.

The fifth feature is implicit in the four already mentioned. The earlier four features presuppose that human creativity and dynamism can serve as a clue or key to the Ultimate Reality or be a "sign of the possibilities and qualities of the creativity manifest within the cosmic process."[60] The creativity of humans (the struggle toward higher and higher levels of humanization and humaneness) shows forth the divine creativity itself in finite, creaturely way. This is what in traditional theology is thought to exemplify the very "image of God."[61]

Sixth, all the five features mentioned in themselves presuppose yet another one. The whole of theological and ethical construction or reconstruction is intended to provide orientation for human beings in the world. Theological-ethical construction is always a vision of human's place in the world and what can facilitate the flourishing of human life. In *ktizonomous* ethics, humans are urged to orient themselves and seek "salvation" by directing human creativity to seek to grasp the Unconditional, by reflecting divine creativity of which it is a part. This will be best done not by consciously directing "autonomy," (*autos nomos*, an "inner law"), not by suppressing the inner dynamism of autonomous cultural creations, and not by an imposition of an alienating law by a theocratic, nationalistic or statist order. It is only an attempt to fully restore the autonomous in historical

---

59. Ibid., 339.
60. Ibid., 138, 266.
61. Ibid., 297.

developments by connecting or reconnecting it to the underlying creativity of which it is a part; to generate an awareness of its depth, a healthy sensitivity to the profound mystery of creativity in its sallying forth. "[*Ktizonomous*] is normative through a deepening of the autonomous, a deepening marked by orienting autonomous forms toward the ultimate, toward the unconditional. This orientation is not… subordination to a norm, but directedness and attraction toward a norm."[62]

Before rounding off the discussions in this section it is germane to give some sense of the unconditional that this essay has persistently placed before the reader. What kind of the unconditional that ethics of emergence as developed in this essay urge the reader to embrace? The unconditional is not the "is" of any situation, nor the "was" of it, but it is "that which is to come." It is the forward straining toward "what is coming and lies in the future," to use the words of Nietzsche who once philosophized creativity both as a principle in cosmology and human psychology (in its manifestations as the "will to power"). This unconditional in itself is devoid of any determinate content. As Bernard Reginster puts it in his evaluation of the Nietzsche's "standard of perfection" in the insatiable move of creativity, "it represents the indeterminate and ever-receding objective of an essentially insatiable creative impulse that is valued for its own sake."[63] In this light, one can then argue that a significant dimension of this unconditional in history simply becomes biohistorical beings' ceaseless "affirmation of becoming itself."

Summary and Concluding Remarks

Kaufman's religious interpretation of emergence as creativity has enabled us to formulate a disciplined cognitive framework for reflecting on ethos of the "profound mystery of creativity." The task of ethical reasoning in this light becomes—no doubt among many others—that of discerning how the deeper dimension of the creative-cultural milieu can be opened up and broadened by orientation to the pervading mystery. This characterization of the task of ethics is an interpretation of five crucial discursive moves that undergird the development of the ethical framework in this essay and the constructive theology that informs it.[64] They are (a) the import of under-

62. Taylor, *Religion, Politics*, 18.
63. Reginster, "Will to Power," 25.
64. Kaufman, *In Face of Mystery*, 297, 339, 358.

standing human existence within the wider cosmic context of life within which it lives, moves, and have its being impels us to ask "how best do we best fit our own projects and activities into the wider and more fundamental movement" of serendipitous creativity?; (b) human life, with its deepest hopes, aspirations and value, is not fundamentally alien to the world, to the created order; (c) in important ways the world in which humans live is "a humane-seeking order;" (d) ongoing human life can and do express "the immediate and continuous presence of the divine creative activity," and (e) the orientation to ultimate creativity, the grounding of human projects in it is believed to give them larger and deeper meaning than is otherwise possible and thus more effectively facilitate the realization of distinctively human potentialities, flourishing, and continuous fulfillment.

CHAPTER FIVE

The Evasion of Ethics: Peter Paris Feels the Spirituals

Opening Word

THIS CHAPTER IS A critical and constructive reflection on the methodology, style, and goal of ethical analysis of Peter Paris, eminent African American ethicist. His approach is to start from the lived experiences of African Americans, putting this ahead of normative reflection, authoritative teachings or divine revelation. Yet there is a theoretical or methodological framework and assumptions that organizes the discourse. Part of my task in this chapter is to unveil the skeleton of the framework for students to see or appropriate for their own scholarship.

This unveiling will also offer practical wisdom on the connections between practices of analysis, habituated and embodied sense of engagement with present situation, and theoretical model of analysis. In this way the seminary student is led to engage with varieties and nuances of ethical analyses as she develops her own voice or style of ethical evaluation.

This chapter shows Paris's work as a model of ethical discourse or "reasoned speech." I want the student to also pay attention to how the discussion of Paris's ethical methodology plays into the format for ethical reasoning or presentation set out in chapter 1. His work is analyzed according to the three-pronged format of chapter 1: (a) statement of the ethical problem that threatens the moral fabric of the American society, (b) the sources of theology and philosophy he brings to bear or shed light on the problem, and (c) solution. His goal is to eliminate racism in the United States. The "ethical widow" he opens for us to see an alternative to the current situation in the United States is clearly highlighted.

Methods of Ethical Analysis

Chapter Introduction

The thesis of this chapter is that Peter Paris evades ethics, meaning he disregards and transcends the dominant ethical theories of the late twentieth and early twenty-first century. He refused to discuss dominant ethical theories and ethical questions abstractly, seeking universally valid principles. Rather, he transitioned from abstract, epistemology-centered ethics to the more contextual approach of comparative and social-problem focused ethics. This inclination in his thought is due to the one all-pervasive evil of racism that casts a shadow on the American society and his native Canada. This evasion of ethics has an affinity with Latin American liberation theology, the dominant theological-ethical paradigm at the time he came of academic age in the 1970s and 1980s. While for liberation theologians the one all-pervasive evil was the capitalist system, for him it was the contempt and discrimination suffered by Black People in the United States and Canada.

The vexing problem that engaged Peter Paris's academic career is racism. In the corpus of his work he has tried to understand and explain the experience of racism and at the same time develop a theological-ethical methodology that is adequate for his subject matter. The aim of the methodology is to unconceal the experience of racism and the responses to it in black religious practices in ways that evade and challenge the American theological enterprise.[1]

> 1. Paris is conscious of the need to develop a methodology for and to express the meaning of his work for black theology. He criticizes James Cone for failing to do this in his work:
> > Cone does not discuss the implication of this study [*Martin and Malcolm*] for theological methodology.... One does not expect a major systematic theologian to write such an important work as this and make virtually no explicit reference to constructive theology. Cone's decision not to explicate the meaning of this book for black theology is very troublesome. (See Paris, "Review of 'Martin & Malcolm,'" 87–90, quote p. 90.)
>
> What Paris means by Cone's failure to explicate the meaning of the book for black theology is not very clear. So I sent an email to him to shed more light on his critique. He responded:
> > My criticism of Cone is that his book is a fine comparative analysis of Malcolm and King; but there is no indication in the book that it is being done by a black theologian. As I read the book I kept waiting to see how these two men related to Cone's black theology project. What do they exemplify in that context? Since neither of them appears to be exemplars of black theology, why does a black theologian choose to write a book about them? Is it that they represent the ambiguity that African American identity entails and which black theology addresses? In any case, Cone does not provide any answers to such questions. Thus I was disappointed with the book because I think he should have told his readers

The Evasion of Ethics: Peter Paris Feels the Spirituals

This chapter not only shows how Paris evades ethics, but it also highlights the creative role of feeling in his work. He is in solidarity with suffering Black People and his anguish has profoundly nourished his intellectual work. His feeling is anchored to the history of slavery, discrimination, and suffering of Blacks in North America and is grounded in a vision of love, hope, equality, and justice.

At their best, his essays exude the rueful lamentation of a "motherless child" mingled with the hope of escape from misery of alienation and degradation to *heaven*.[2] Like the old spirituals, Paris's ethical analyses are conversations with America about blacks' experience of pain and suffering, struggle and striving, and the unity of protest and hope in their religious thought—all carried out in plaintive tones and sad rhythms.[3] With the simplicity of his prose, precision and clarity of thought, and the evocative power of his analytical descriptions, his essays have a mournful beauty to them.

In doing all this Paris avoided being driven and tossed by the winds of flavor-of-the-period philosophies and theories, especially those from Europe that easily beset and beguiled lesser self-controlled and self-confident ethicists in the four decades that he actively thought, researched, and wrote. Not so moved, he endured in his task of rendering in concrete (never abstract and highfalutin) terms the experience of racism. For Paris, ethics is about identifying concrete problems that threaten the moral fabric of a community and seeking to address them with the best of theological, philosophical, and social scientific resources. And the goal of good ethical reasoning is to advance human flourishing. As he puts it in the introductory lecture of his 2008 Harvard University course on the "Ethics and Politics in Black America":

> In my perspective, ethics always takes as its point of departure some concrete actions, deeds, practices performed by persons or groups of persons. In this sense, ethics is always empirical and its aim is to discern the nature of the good or the right or the appropriate inherent in some actual occasion and to describe its limits

---

how these men related to his central project which is the construction of black theology. (Paris, e-mail message to author, April 14, 2010.)

2. For his understanding of heaven or rather the notion of heaven in the spirituals as a principle of social criticism, see Paris, "When Feeling Like a Motherless Child," 113; Paris, "Linguistic Inculturation," 80–81, 89–90; Paris, "Problem of Evil," 304.

3. I have adapted Paris's words from "When Feeling Like a Motherless Child," 115–16, for my purposes here.

and possibilities; i.e., what values are sacrificed or not allowed to see the light of day and the difference it would make were things to be otherwise.[4]

The primary concrete problems of the United States are lingering racism and poverty and ethicists must endeavor to inform thinking on them. In the twentieth century the color line, in the language of W. E. B. Du Bois, was the problem. In the twenty-first century it is still here, but Paris adds to it "poverty both at home and abroad."[5] Social ethicists of the twenty-first century must aim at expanding and enhancing moral community by eliminating all obstacles to life, eradicating policies, institutions, and patterns of behavior that thwart flourishing life.

In thinking about racism and poverty, several questions preoccupied Paris for nearly half a century. How can the moral problems of racism and poverty be solved? How can the social structures that sustain them be changed for the good of the oppressed, marginalized, and poor persons? What have been the thoughtful public responses of African Americans to these problems? Did the responses arise from how American citizens (both black and white) deliberately and intentionally worked to reorder human relations so as to include those excluded from participating at the bounteous table of this great nation? For him, social ethics begins when the citizens of a country start reasoned discourses about the quality of the human relations, actions, and practices that sustain the problems that threaten their society's moral fabric, with a view to reordering society for the better. His publications have captured some of the most reasoned discourses of African American leaders on racism and poverty. In this Parisian way of approaching the social problems faced by African Americans, ethics and politics are inseparable.

Though trained in major philosophical and theological discourses of the twentieth century, as well as ancient Greek thought (especially that of Aristotle), much of Paris's creative thinking has drawn strength and direction from the struggle for freedom and justice in his African American heritage. The primary aspects of this heritage that inform his work are its politics and ethics. The politics of African Americans is the ethical critique of the American society in order to create a flourishing life for blacks in this country; not only for them but for all Americans. Du Bois stated this clearly in *The Souls of Black Folks* by stating that one of the three important gifts

---

4. Paris, "Ethics and Politics," 4.
5. Paris, "African-American Religion," 487.

The Evasion of Ethics: Peter Paris Feels the Spirituals

of blacks to the United States is ethical critique of the society to expose its moral limits, to remind it of its blindnesses and silences in white America's reflections on the nation's problems, and to enhance its morality.[6]

According to Paris, "African American political leaders have been forced by the nature of their primary concerns to keep the moral problem of racism clearly visible on the political agenda. And that has constituted their unique contribution to the nation's moral life."[7] Paris's work has therefore focused on making visible to the world the oppression of blacks that has been systematically and carefully concealed from the public; but more importantly, the gallant ways blacks have responded to their oppression with virtues of love, forgiveness, and redemption or reconciliation.

With this sort of cultural investigation or academic approach to America's social crises, some scholars may be led to argue that Paris has not done ethics, but evaded it. He avoids ontological abstractions, metaphysical language, or philosophic speculation, but always looks carefully into areas of human experience in which resistance to injustice and passion for actualization of creative potentials play are central. For instance, while others may write tomes on how racism is socially constructed and historically constituted, he will prefer to expose the structures of oppression and profile blacks' experience of it and their responses to alter their situation.

Paris converts ethics into a positive science of social critique. He insists both in his classroom lectures and academic publications that such a critique must be specific and particular. For him the nature of such critique—and for that matter, ethics—is to discern the nature and dynamics of the threats to human flourishing in every particular sociality. And this it can only do in direct confrontation with concrete, present threats to the moral fabric of the sociality, and never as abstract analysis or argument, never in advance or once and for all.

For him, this commitment to ethics as defeasible and incompletable—as social critique—means that one cannot set down a definitive method for doing ethics or replicating any major work of ethics. Paris does not want to convert concrete criticism into a philosophy of social science (humanities) or a paradigmatic methodology. For him, neither social criticism nor the process of gathering facts and assessing values about a particular configuration of social relations can or need be totalized.

---

6. Du Bois, *Soul of Black Folks*, 205, 214–16. See also West, *American Evasion of Philosophy*, 143.

7. Paris, "Ethics and Politics," 5.

Methods of Ethical Analysis

My interpretation of Paris's work as an evasion of ethics demands a more sustained argument, as this will enable me to show the prophetic dimension of his scholarship, which is a key to understanding his commitment to ethics as social critique. I use the word *prophetic* in the special sense given by Cornel West: "The basic contribution of prophetic Christianity, despite the countless calamities perpetrated by Christian churches, is that every individual regardless of class, country, caste, race, or sex should have the opportunity to fulfill his or her potentialities."[8]

The Evasion of Ethics

There are ethicists who do ethics and there is Paris who does ethics by evading ethics. Those in the first group engage in the following kinds of ethics. There is epistemology-centered ethics; that is meta-ethical views of cognitivism and noncognitivism. These involve inquiry into or debate about the basis of objective moral knowledge. There is theory-centered ethics, in which scholars fiercely debate whether ethics is truly about duty (obedience to law) or telos to be achieved (or aimed at). Yet others debate the merits and demerits of general theories or proper definition of words like *good*, *right*, or *virtues*. There are also ethicists who are committed to the bifurcation of the "ought" and the "is" and see its violation as accenting to the "vulgar systems of morality." There are still others who work from facts or common knowledge and from such derive some ultimate principle. Finally, there are scholars working to provide a full, systematic method of doing ethics. The most common thread of these approaches to ethics is that they are removed from the practical, urgent problems of society. Their advocates pride themselves in transcending the quotidian human struggles for identity, dignity, freedom, and survival.

Peter Paris evades all these by turning away from the wispy cloud of theories floating as a halo over the earth to stand firm on the terra-firma of actual moral problems. His orientation is to illuminate practical problems by forcing theories to touch the ground. As most of his former doctoral students will attest, Paris will listen patiently to a brilliant presentation, wearing a smile of approval, only to ask with the intense concentration of an Olympic gymnast on a slim iron bar, "where do all these touch the ground?"[9] An ethical work touches the ground when it is on the side of

8. West, *Prophesy Deliverance*, 16.
9. I was a doctoral student of Paris's at Princeton Theological Seminary, Princeton.

The Evasion of Ethics: Peter Paris Feels the Spirituals

human freedom and affirms human flourishing in its broadest sense. It can only do so when it starts by focusing on concrete problems and finding ways to liberate the agents trapped in them. Thus he declares:

> An inquiry in social ethics should begin with some actual, concrete problems arising among human beings in their public actions. That is to say, such an investigation should begin with some conflicting views about the good that humans can and should do.... The result of such an investigation should be some resolution of the problem or a restatement of the problem in order to liberate the agents and their activities and to establish thereby the conditions for more creative enterprise.[10]

The primary theme of Paris's work is evading epistemology-centered ethics (conscience-centered, fundamentals-centered, revelation-centered, or philosophic/biblical absolutism), exposing racism and injustice, and accenting the transformation of the structures of domination and subordination in the light of an ethical ideal, which is usually the thwarting of evil or actualization of human potentialities.[11] The far-reaching appeal of his thought lies in its commitment to social and cultural criticism, moral emphasis, and vitality for transformation. For Paris social ethics is a form of cultural criticism, cultural investigation of injustice, and the clarification of its solutions in the light of a religious and/or ethical ideal.

His preoccupation with evading ethics determines his methodology of ethical analysis or argumentation. His ethical analysis starts with a definition of the problem or a description of the ethical concern. Once the problem is adequately identified and laid out, he will undertake a social scientific examination of it and then provide a theological-ethical interpretation. Next he will point his readers to likely solutions to the problem that is threatening the moral fabric of the given community. The accent of the solution is always political, on reordering of the human relations in the community.

He sees every solution, whether suggested by him or inherited, as ultimately subject to the law of transformation in history. In this light every institution and tradition—especially the ones that buoy up racism, injustice, and poverty—are dissolvable by the power of this law that holds them fluid, protean, and dynamic. Human relations may be perfect for a

---

10. Paris, *Black Religious Leaders*, 31–32.

11. This way of interpreting Paris's work was fueled by intellectual stimulus I got from West, *American Evasion of Philosophy*.

historical moment, but are never complete. All social practices or ordering of human relations are revisable and contingent. He argues that "societies are not natural constructs. They were designed and built by humans and each one could have been different than it is. They are not controlled by the laws of nature even though they are subject to certain natural conditions that place some limits on their aspirations."[12]

Paris took the path that swerves from mainline ethics not because he wanted to be different, but because he only wanted to be faithful to the concerns of his black community and its understanding of ethics. His evasion of ethics is, therefore, seen as an embrace of an African-American tradition that stridently resists white racism, a life threatening situation:

> Suffice it to say that ethics in the black community has racism as its subject matter; i.e., human action that views race as a significant condition for preserving and enhancing privileges for one group and the corresponding denial of such privileges to the excluded group. . . . Ethics in the black community has not been a speculative enterprise. Rather, it has been concrete, experiential, practical and deeply rooted in the realities of racial conflict.[13]

He not only believes that racism is the subject matter of black ethics, but that it should have been the main subject matter of American theological enterprise in the last century. Thus, when asked to evaluate the first hundred years of Catholic social teaching in America he began his response by saying, "Since racial injustice has been the paramount reality for African-American existence for over four centuries, no adequate evaluation of the Christian churches in general, or the Catholic Church in particular, can be undertaken apart from this fact."[14]

Accordingly, the celebrated Christian theologians and ethicists of the twentieth century who avoided the race question cannot be deemed the greatest of American theologians. He boldly nominates Martin Luther King and James Cone as the worthiest of all American theologians in the twentieth century:

> In my judgment, Martin Luther King, Jr., and James H. Cone are the two major American theologians of the twentieth century, black or white. The most significant similarity between the two is their respective understandings of the relationship of the Christian

12. Paris, "Ethics and Politics," 3.
13. Ibid., 6.
14. Paris, "Catholic Social Teaching," 299.

The Evasion of Ethics: Peter Paris Feels the Spirituals

gospel to the struggle for racial justice in the United States. . . . Clearly, neither King nor Cone engaged in speculative theology concerning the nature of God nor did they participate in much academic discourse about classical doctrines of faith. Rather, their theologies served the practical purpose of effecting racial justice. Each believed that the truth of the gospel is evidenced in its capacity to restore wholeness to a broken community. Hence, it was imperative for them that theology be integrally related to the concrete issues of social injustice in general and to the pursuit of racial justice in particular. Each viewed theology as prophetic because Jesus was a prophet.[15]

Anyone who has read Paris's book *The Spirituality of African Peoples*, which deals with the virtues of African-Americans, might contend that in it he was not successful in completely evading virtue ethics in particular. The virtue school of ethics derives from Plato and Aristotle and it is a bastion of mainline ethics. In anticipation of this kind of criticism, Paris flagged his credentials of evasion by first cutting a swath of difference between him and modern virtue ethicists; then between him and Aristotle, whose inductive method of inquiry characterizes aspects of this book.

Paris states that "many modern virtue ethicists have much in common with the Platonic and Augustinian tradition. My approach, however, differs from theirs in being more closely related to the Aristotelian tradition."[16] What he evades is Plato's notion of virtues that are ideal forms and the Augustinian view of "moral life as faith in Jesus Christ and obedience to the dictates of God."[17] For him, the virtues of this approach are in wispy clouds, far above the struggles of human beings. He wants to bring them back to the ground. "By identifying God with the true end of human action, ethics becomes deductive inquiry that begins with the being of God rather that the strivings of humans. From this line of Platonic thinking the Christian virtues were understood as supernatural and transcendental of human strivings."[18]

In the case of Aristotle, he maintains that there are only a small number of methodological similarities between the ethics of African Americans and that of the great philosopher. Yet he admits that an Aristotelian shadow haunts many parts of his text. This is only because Aristotle's theory of

15. Paris, "Comparing the Public Theologies," 220–21.
16. Paris, *Spirituality of African Peoples*, 183n7.
17. Ibid., 182n7.
18. Ibid.

moral virtue has enormous influence on the development of moral theories. Nonetheless, he lets us know that he tried very hard to swerve from the path Aristotle carved out for mainline ethics: "I have made every effort to stay within the thought forms of the latter [Africans and African-Americans] throughout this study. In my judgment, any structural similarities between Aristotle's ethical thought and that of Africans and African-American should not be viewed as another instance of Western epistemological imperialism since the content of the African and African-American ethic is decidedly culturally specific."[19]

His commitment to evading ethics as it was understood or executed by the leading ethicist of the past four decades also colored his understanding of political power. Since he viewed theology and ethics as practical sciences in the service of one's community's well-being—academic enterprises pursued for the sake of revealing practical solutions for everyday problems—he regarded them as "intrinsically political." This view flows from his understanding of the black church tradition:

> The Black churches have always had profound concern for the bitter and painful realities of black existence in America as a well as for a bright and radiant future (eschaton) free from any form of racial injustice. The latter designates the locus of ultimate value where all people are in harmony with the transcendent, holy, and supreme God of the Judeo-Christian faith. Traditionally, the Black churches have interpreted human life, including all its suffering and pain, in accordance with that ultimate goal in which they have never lost faith. The convergence of that sacred principle with their efforts for improved temporal conditions reveals the integral relationship of religion and politics in the Black churches.[20]

He thus rejects the ethics of Stanley Hauerwas whose work explicitly rejects "direct responsibility for political engagement."[21]

In conclusion, Paris evades twentieth-century ethics, first by rejecting epistemology-centered, knowledge-focus problematic of modern ethics. For him, ethical problems are linked to social crises and quotidian human struggles for selfhood, identity, and power in specific communities. He does not see theological ethics as a form of knowledge or a means of acquiring knowledge, but as efforts to address and ameliorate social

---

19. Ibid., 183n8.
20. Paris, "Social World," 1–16, quote pp. 1–2.
21. Paris, *Spirituality of African Peoples*, 132, 182n6.

problems. Second, he avoids the quest for philosophical respectability and theological sophistication, preferring to apply theological ethics to the historical interpretation of race relations. Third, he skillfully refuses theology or philosophy's search for enduring, universal truths. He argues, "Morality pertains to the cultural ethos and, hence, is culturally specific. According to this perspective, there is a no universal morality as such, even though some common moral values are widespread among diverse cultural groups. Yet in my judgment morality is univocal only within particular communities. That is to say, it is determined by the norms, values, and goals of particular communities."[22] And finally, he exposes Western theology's affiliation with whites' privileges and romance with structures of power.[23]

Intellectual Roots of Paris's Ethics

My effort to interpret Paris as evading ethics should neither imply parochialism nor suggests that his work is ahistorically *novum*. He is not a Melchizedek without father or mother or ancestors. Neither is he an Athena who burst forth from her father Zeus' forehead, fully mature. He drank deeply from some of the major intellectual arrowheads of twentieth-century theology, ethics, and philosophy. A close reading of his works easily reveals that their roots burrow into the minds of Aristotle, Paul Tillich, Reinhold and Richard Niebuhr, Ernst Troeltsch, and Hannah Arendt, to mention only a few.

In learning from and in appropriating the thoughts of these great thinkers, he always put a question mark behind them. For him, these thinkers never dealt adequately with racism, with the death-dealing evil of structural marginalization and exclusion. In a discussion with him, he will accept the influences of these scholars on his thinking, but he is likely to evade any attempt to push him too closely to them. He thinks that the African-American tradition of ethics and politics is the predominant influence on his thought. This much is clear to him, and he thinks this influence is even predominant in the thoughts of even those African-American theologians who do not explicitly reflect on the religious heritage of African Americans and its power on their creative thinking and acting. He will put

---

22. Ibid., 134. See also Paris, "Moral Development," 23.

23. On this see in particular his piece on Kuyper; Paris, "African and African-American Understanding," 263–80.

Martin Luther King Jr. in this category, quoting the authority of Cone to buttress his point:

> Thus much of King's writings reflect theological and philosophical discourses that had little to do with his actual creative thinking and acting. The source of the latter is not Gandhi or Bostonian personalism, despite his implied claims to the contrary. King's creative thought and power in the struggle of freedom were found in his black heritage. This was the heritage that brought him face to face with agony and despair but also hope and joy that somewhere in the bosom of God's eternity, justice would become a reality "in the land of the free and the home of the brave." This was the source of King's dream and his anticipation that "trouble won't last always."[24]

In spite of all this demurring, we can still trace the powerful influences of other traditions on Paris's thought, including that of Aristotle, Tillich, Niebuhr, Troeltsch, Arendt, liberation theology, and social science method in his thought, even if these influences are only remote.

From Aristotle he learned the craft of ethics as an inductive and empirical inquiry into the ethos of particular communities. The scholar starts with concrete problems—investigating what is actually happening in society, what is undermining the good—and ends with the creation of capabilities, virtues, and polis to ensure the good. Incidentally, Paris taught the *Nicomachean Ethics* and *Politics* of Aristotle as a doctoral seminar at Princeton Theological Seminary for decades.

If the empirical, inductive method comes from Aristotle, Paris's style of relating ethical analysis to concrete problem comes from his teacher, Paul Tillich, and his *Correlation Method*. A theological-ethical analysis must deal with the questions people are asking and address them with resources of the faith. Simply, the ethicist is to correlate problems and questions with resources, myths, and symbols of their faith to address them. Not only does he take this approach in his study, it also informs the way he treats his subjects. He presents them as expert in doing this. Take, for instance his 1985 book, *The Social Teaching of the Black Churches*, where he uses the categories of ordinary folks (pastors and denominational leaders) outside the academe. He tried to weave a theology (more precisely, theological ethics/religious social ethics) from their actions and words in reaction to racism

---

24. Cone, *God of the Oppressed*, 221–22, quoted in Paris, "Comparing the Public Theologies," 226. See also Noll, *God and Race*, 107–23.

and other environmental conditions. The theology of the black churches he constructed, therefore, is not supernatural, transcendental of human strivings. In this is the sense, it does not stand above and outside of the collective praxis of blacks. His strength is his capacity to relate theological ethics to the structured and unstructured social practices of blacks in America over the past two hundred years—from when David George founded the first black church in the United States to the present era.[25]

In this potent brew of theological ingredients, we need to add a dash of Niebuhr to give some flavor. Niebuhr once said that anyone answering questions that have not been asked is foolish. He also argues that we must pay attention to self-interest and power imbalance in our ethical analyses. Paris in *Social Teaching* and in all of his other books always addresses the questions that blacks in the United States are asking. Niebuhr's "realism" is also evident in his work. In *Social Teaching*, the reader will notice a succinct analysis of imbalance of power and injustice, men and women in immoral society, the self-interests of the dominant and oppressed groups, and occasional dialectics of argument in presenting the reaction of blacks to racism. Paris not only taught courses on Niebuhr and his brother Richard for many years, he is also an active member of the Niebuhr Society right from its inception.[26] He calls himself "a Niebuhrian pragmatist," without necessarily accenting the aspects of Niebuhr's Christian realism that advised African Americans to be cautious and patient in their demand to eradicate racial injustice as they must endeavor to take into account all other factors.[27]

This revelation of his pragmatic bend is very important in understanding the direction his work has taken: ethical problems as linked to societal problems, conceptions of ethics as struggles over a societal ordering of human relations and cultural ways of life, and the rethinking of ethics as a form of cultural criticism for flourishing of human progress and moral enhancement of societies. As West has argued in *The American Evasion of Philosophy*, the evasion of epistemology-centered philosophy—in the thought of American thinkers such like James Dewey, Du Bois, Reinhold Niebuhr—

> [R]esults in conception of philosophy as a form of cultural criticism in which the meaning of America is put forward by

25. For the story of David George see Paris, "David George," 2–9.
26. Paris, "Response to Langdon Gilkey's," 475–79.
27. Paris, e-mail message to author, February 26, 2009. See also Paris, "Moral Development," 24.

Methods of Ethical Analysis

intellectuals in response to distinct social and cultural crises. In this sense, American pragmatism is less a philosophical [ethical] tradition putting forward solutions to perennial problems in the Western philosophical conversation initiated by Plato and more a continuous commentary or set of interpretations that attempt to explain America to itself at a particular historical moment.[28]

Paris is Troeltschian in his execution of his project, especially in *The Social Teaching of the Black Churches*. "I think that the title of [this] book gives a strong preference for the spirit of Troeltsch because I wanted to emphasize the force of God's parenthood and human kinship as the primary counteracting force against the racist agenda of the nation at large and the white churches in particular. As such that principle constitutes the raison d'etre of the black churches which represents its institutionalization."[29] Troeltsch, the German theologian of the late nineteen and early twentieth century, presented in his influential book, *The Social Teaching of the Christian Churches*, the ethics of Christian churches as an investigation into how religious ideas and social interests are (become) congruent. His goal was to show how religious ideas agree with actual, material reality; what are the compromises (co-promising deals) that have been made to achieve the Church's interest since religious ideals cannot be fully realized in society. This encounter of religious ideas and social reality is the realm of social teaching. Troeltsch developed three "ideal types" of religious organizations: Church, sect, and mystic. The Church is the only one of the three capable of adapting the original religious idea to hard material and social interest to produce a social teaching. It is capable of making compromises in the public realm.

Richard Niebuhr's *Christ and Culture* was influenced by Troeltsch's "ideal types" which in turn influenced Paris's use of the biblical leadership ideals of prophet, priest, and king in his first book *Black Religious Leaders*." Also Richard's book *The Responsible Self* influenced Paris's understanding of blacks as agents who respond to God's initiative toward them. That response begins with interpreting the action that they confront before responding in accordance with God's purpose for humanity. Like Richard Niebuhr, Paris is also an ethicist engaged with hermeneutics, social science, theology, and history in doing Christian social ethics. All this are very evident in his *Black Religious Leaders* and the *Social Teaching of the Black Churches*.

In his analysis of the social teaching of the black churches, Paris accented political actions as the originative, sustaining basis, and even the

28. West, *American Evasion of Philosophy*, 5.
29. Paris, email message to author, February 26, 2009.

subject matter of social ethics.³⁰ This move to accent political action is not totally innocent or arbitrary. One sees the influence of Arendt, one of his favorite philosophers. In her influential 1958 book, *The Human Condition*, she shows that political actions, deeds, and speeches in the public realm, have the function of disclosing and affirming identity of agents—who they are, not what they are. They reveal themselves as the unique individuals that they are. The political or the polis is the "space of appearance" where people appear to one another as they come together to undertake common projects. For her, power (not strength, force, or violence), the main instrument of the political realm, arises when persons act in concert for a common public-political purpose. Thus, both the polis as the space of appearance and power as an outcome of collective engagement are always potential and are actualized in actions and speeches of persons who act in concert for a common public project. In her view, the analysis of the political or social-ethical should be focused on the public space. This is again reflected in Paris's works as he has overwhelmingly focused on political leaders acting in the public realm.

There is another way Arendt influenced him. As we have already shown in the analysis of the nature and meaning of history in the black churches, he limited himself to political actions. To my chagrin as an economic ethicist, he ignores economic actions.³¹ More correctly, he subsumes economics under politics. This preference reflects the subtle influence of Arendt on his thinking.³² (Though she is not directly mentioned in the book, I know,

---

30. Paris, *Social Teaching*, 2–3.

31. When I queried him about this he responded in this way:
    I am sorry about the lack of any attention to the economic sphere. I thought a great deal about that and decided to leave it out because it seemed to me that the black churches did not pay much attention to it apart from beginning various micro businesses that displayed no thought that was different from the status quo of the day.

    Previously, I had worked closely with Jesse Jackson in the early days of his work in Chicago when his program Operation Breadbasket was the economic arm of Martin Luther King's SCLC. Apart from opposing the racism in the many big businesses that refused to employ blacks while readily taking their cash, neither King nor Jackson displayed any novel economic thought. When the book is revised I think that perhaps I now need to say something about this matter and would welcome your insights.

    You are certainly right in discerning that I view politics as prior to economics even though the state needs a material basis as a necessary condition. (Paris, email message to author, February 26, 2009).

32. This tendency may also have been influenced by Aristotle who viewed economics as a household responsibility and, hence, outside of the political realm. It is needless,

Methods of Ethical Analysis

as his former student, his love for her thought.) He appears to be working from her schema of *labor, work,* and *action*. In *labor* and *work*, people only show their talents, abilities, deficiencies, and shortcomings. What she calls labor is necessitated by the demands of biological survival. There is no room for uniqueness or distinction. We are all the same insofar as we are parts of the human species chained to natural necessities, the needs of the body. The products of *labor* do not last—they are very short-lived. Here, the criterion of judgment is the ability to sustain human life. In *work*, the situation is slightly different. We are able to show some individuality, our products bear some distinctive marks, but the maker is subordinated to the end product and the product will outlive him or her. The end product tells us very little about the maker except that he or she has certain skills and capabilities. The criterion of judgment is the ability to create a world fit for human existence. In *actions*, in relating and interacting with others, without intermediary matter or things, for common purpose, persons disclose and affirm their unique identities and actualize their capacities for freedom. Actions have the potentials to introduce the *novum* and the totally unexpected into the world. This potential cannot be actualized in isolation from others who are there to work in concert with us and/or to judge the quality of what is being stated and/or enacted. The criterion of judgment is the capacity to reveal unique identities and introduce the new, a novelty into the world; to expect the unexpected. Blacks needed to reach this level of living, which for Arendt is the *differentia specifica* of human life. In Paris's theology, political action is what will affirm their claim as being created in the image of God and what will differentiate them from the life of animals and objects of possession, which was their lot under white slave masters.

The affinity with Arendt's thought, notwithstanding, Paris is quick to distance himself from aspects of her theory of power in the public realm:

> I love Hannah Arendt's understanding of the public realm even though I shun some of the elitism that attends it and see no reason why it could not be less elitist than it seems to be. I also am more a Niebuhrian pragmatist than she in seeing an important ethical role for power as a corrective to the wrong use of power. Also, I think Niebuhr's view of sin is more realistic than her seeming lack thereof even though her view of Totalitarianism fits very nicely with Niebuhr's view of sin."[33]

---

to say that Arendt also worked of from Aristotelian ideas.

33. Ibid.

Liberation theology is another influence on his thought.[34] For him, practice is prior to thought in theological-ethical reflection. Even though it is less in vogue these days, he still holds onto one of its valuable insights: the purpose of theological or ethical analysis to liberate people from oppression. Though working within the liberation theology paradigm, Paris did not see it necessary to develop any systematic connection between racism and economic injustice in the United States in the ways that, for example, Cornell West has been able to do.

Finally, Paris uses a lot of social scientific data and archival research to analyze the history and distinctive identity of African-Americans. As was related to this writer the reliance on the social scientific method comes from his doctoral training at the University of Chicago Divinity School in the 1960s. He feels very strongly about the place of the social sciences in theological education, even advocating that seminary students spend "as much as a year's study in university disciplines or programs considered relevant to [their] professional needs" in order to be adequately prepared for the people and the country they will serve.[35]

The value of social analysis in theology and ethics is deliberately keyed to his hermeneutics derived from his commitment to liberation theology. He is impatient with scholars who profess doing liberation theology while ignoring social analysis. This much is revealed in his review of Cone's 1991 book, *Martin and Malcolm and America: A Dream or a Nightmare*. Trenchantly, Paris criticizes his friend:

> Throughout his career Cone's work has been criticized for its lack of social analysis. The subject of this book could have provided an excellent opportunity for the possible correction of that deficit. Seemingly, Cone refused to accept the challenge. Rather, by employing a narrative approach he has analyzed a cultural phenomenon in such a way as to obscure the political dimension of the social problem. This is especially problematic for black theology, which has always claimed to be a political theology deeply rooted in the praxis of liberation. Cone does not tell us how this analysis helps in liberating blacks from their present condition.[36]

---

34. See Paris, "Religious Social Ethics," 135–145; Paris, "Character of Liberation Ethics," 133–140; Paris, "Womanist Thought," 115–26.

35. Paris, "Overcoming Alienation," 194.

36. Paris, "Review of 'Martin & Malcolm,'" 90.

Methods of Ethical Analysis

Paris's Ethical Methodology

The ethical methodology of Paris can be summarized as an intersection of eight key insights. First, the good of the public realm or social is measured by the full actualization of human potentialities.[37] According to him, "the purpose of ethics is to enhance the quality of human action by enabling people to actualize their full potentialities."[38] This concern with actualization of potentials is scattered all through his works.[39] Start from where he is analyzing forms and approaches to racism in the *Black Religious Leaders*, that is, the approach of black religious leaders in adjusting the ideals of the Bible to American reality; move over to an account of their efforts to realize biblical ideals in America in the *Social Teaching*; then shift your gaze to where he is looking at the spirituality of African peoples, and you will discover that his great concern (implicit and explicit—often implicit) has always been about what is blocking the unfolding of the potentialities of blacks in America. How can they overcome obstacles to actualization of their potentialities, or how are (were) their traditional (African and African-American) forms of sociality organized so that a black person can be all that he or she can be—can experience full human flourishing?

Second, the focus of his ethical analysis is on finding out what is threatening the moral fabric of the society, especially in ways that inhibit the actualization of potentialities of persons and their community as a whole and then addressing it in ways that can remove the threats.[40] He examined the interplay between politics (the ordering of human relations in a society) and the part of life we call spiritual or religious as lived—not as argued. The weight of his work always tilts toward empirical facts, observable social practices rather than theory. Take, for instance, his major academic concern with racism. He does not engage in theoretical debate about the nature or origin of racism, but he lets his subjects reveal their understanding of it and he then tries to capture their responses and resistance to it.

Third, there is a good mixture of social scientific and historical methods at work in his scholarly output. Most good ethicists employ social science methods and insights in their works; but very few resort to the craft of

---

37. Paris, *Social Teaching*, 2, 58–59, 115–16.
38. Paris, "Is it Moral," 51.
39. For instance, see Paris, "Social World," 2; Paris, "Justice and Mercy," 222; Paris, "Bible and the Black Churches," 140.
40. Paris, *Black Religious Leaders*, 31–32.

The Evasion of Ethics: Peter Paris Feels the Spirituals

the historian to do ethics. Paris goes into archives to ferret out and interpret historical records. He is comfortable with employing the research skills and the principles and methods of historical analysis. Especially in the *Social Teaching of the Black Churches* the reader can easily notice the excellent use of primary and secondary sources in interpreting the theological responses of black churches to racism.

Fourth, every person needs a community *(communal eros)* to become fully human and to fully actualize his or her potentialities as an American citizen. If this is denied a group of persons, they are bound to form a substitute one. The systematic and society-wide racism that African Americans experienced resulted in their loss of place and in becoming exiled within their own country. Racism also denied blacks the process and opportunity for self-actualization. The Church became a surrogate community. "Since it is necessary for persons to be nourished by a communal eros in order to become fully human, an imposed exile necessitates the formation of a substitute community, and, as we have seen, that has been one of the major functions of the black churches."[41] In another place, he states that:

> A fundamental assumption underlying my understanding of social ethics is the dialectical relationship between person and community. That is to say, personhood is established only in the context of a community of persons that in turn constitutes both a limiting condition and a liberating resource for all thought and practice. Similarly, community is constituted when persons choose to come together to create, preserve, and enhance the conditions that make possible their common life.[42]

Fifth, ethics cannot be separated from politics. He states that "ethics and politics are integrally united. The aim of ethics is to help persons become morally good, and the aim of politics is the same."[43] And he would add that without the strong foundation and interplay between ethics and politics neither the individual nor his or her community cannot actualize their full potentialities.

It is quite tempting to wholly attribute Paris's insistence on the interweaving of ethics and politics to his self-professed embrace of neo-Aristotelianism. After all, Aristotle had theorized the close connection between ethics and politics. It might also be tempting to interpret Paris's inclination

41. Paris, *Social Teaching*, 59–61, quote p. 59.
42. Paris, "Moral Development," 23–32.
43. Ibid., 25.

as solely arising from his location as an African American. After all, most white theologians and ethicists avoid writing about racism.[44] The better (additional) argument as far as his methodology is concerned is his focus on concrete problems. After all, many American theologians who are also neo-Aristotelian have not made racial injustice and the struggles against it the pivot of their scholarship and social activism. Early in his academic career, Paris set his eyes on focusing on concrete problems, the major problems that threaten the moral fabric of the American society, the agency of blacks in resisting them, and the black Churches' response to them.[45] He thus set race and politics as the key components of American ethical life and the pivot of his scholarship. By doing this Paris latched onto the most profound moral problem of this country. As the famed historian Mark A. Noll informs us in his 2008 book, *God and Race in American Politics*:

> First, race has always been among the most influential elements in American political history, and in many periods absolutely the most influential. Second, religion has always been crucial for the workings of race in American politics. Together, race and religion make up, not only the nation's deepest and most enduring moral problem, but also its broadest and most enduring political influence.[46]

Sixth, there is always an indication in his work that it is done by a black theologian. He consciously expresses the meaning of all his work for constructing black theology. When he writes about personalities like Martin Luther King Jr., Malcolm X, Joseph H. Jackson, Adam Powell Jr., David George, James Cone, or institutions like the black Churches, he endeavors to show how what they do exemplify the black religious tradition. He asks and answers this basic question of what they do represent in terms of the ambiguity that African-American identity entails and that black theology addresses?[47]

Seventh, Paris writes from the vantage point of the victims of American history. He is aware that he was not only thinking and writing about America's most enduring moral problem, but also about the "strange experience of being a problem."[48] Paris turned Western theological tradition

---

44. Cone, "Theology's Great Sin," 139–52.
45. See Paris, "David George."
46. Noll, *God and Race*, 1.
47. See discussion in footnote 1 of this chapter for details.
48. Du Bois, *Soul of Black Folks*, 3–4.

The Evasion of Ethics: Peter Paris Feels the Spirituals

inside out by not simply legitimizing the capacity of its ethical reasoning to overcome the profound moral problem of America, but more importantly, by asking over and over again how it feels to be a problem[49]— a problem that America has ignored for too long, that its white theologians are reluctant to face squarely to develop "antiracist theologies that go beyond simply condemning racism because they engage the histories, cultures and theologies of people of color."[50] The aim of Paris's ethical discourse is to "convey and enact the 'strange experience' of 'being a problem'":[51] that is, being an ethicist of African descent in America and refusing to measure the black experience by "the tape of a world that looks on in amused contempt and pity."[52] He is able to pull this off without having "double consciousness"[53] in his professional identity and status.

Finally, it is important to mention that Paris does not only focus on African American as victims. More importantly, he has demonstrated in all his work that African Americans have been agents throughout their history and not merely victims. Victims are acted upon. They do not act. Agents respond and do something about their situation. Their agency reveals their subjectivity and hence, their humanity. This is a fact, he believes, took American whites a long, long time to affirm.

Concluding Remarks

On the whole, the extensity and intensity of Paris's conception and method of ethics suggests that he is a scholar who evades modern theological ethics as we know it. This evasion is pursued so as to render, in my judgment, his academic work as a form of the *spirituals*. He wants his audience to feel the pathos and passion of centuries of oppression of blacks in this country. To fully appreciate his work the reader needs to feel the sorrow and the hope that are embedded in the descriptions and analyses of racial injustice and

---

49. This is a paraphrase of West's turn of phrase in *American Evasion of Philosophy*, 142.
50. Cone, "Theology's Great Sin," 139.
51. West, *American Evasion of Philosophy*, 142.
52. Du Bois, *Soul of Black Folks*, 5.
53. As a citizen he may have "double consciousness" in so far as he is an African-American, but here I am talking about double consciousness in his work and identity as a black scholar. He is not trying to locate his scholarship simultaneously in two worlds or let himself be measured by the tape of those who want to sweep racism under the academic rug or both evade and affirm the constricted Western theological enterprise.

responses to it. For him, the capacity to feel (written by the one who feels them and hoping in turn to make his readers feel them as well) is more important than any display of erudition and obeisance to Western theological tradition. The eros for justice and political engagement in all concrete relational contexts requires some passion.

The evasion and the *feel* that characterize Paris's fierce ethical engagement with white racism and Western theological tradition are interwoven and jointly arise from his deep and profound understanding of the spirituals. He considers the spiritual as the "primary repository of African-American theological thought."[54] These slave songs in their linguistic format of double entendre evaded the slave masters' theology, panoptic gaze, and intrusive ears only to unleash passions for everyday resistance and give courage to those who had the *hearts* to hear their concealed messages. Our master-teacher Paris, like the unnamed bards of the spirituals, countless great black preachers, and brave black activists drew from the same ethos formed by a deep concern for oppression and liberation. This concern, according to our learned professor, is (should be) the central focus of the Gospel and theological ethics. And it is what drives his commitment to ethics.

The first major weakness of Paris's ethical thought is his consistent and persistent focus on a single unifying category for American social ethics—racism—when ethics needs to be more comprehensive.[55] Has he reduced

54. Paris, "Linguistic Inculturation," 80.
55. I asked Paris to defend himself about this charge and this is what he had to say: I wonder why it should be a major weakness that I have focused my work on racism. I have done so because it is the primary ethical problem in the American situation since racism denies people their humanity. It is a frontal attack on their humanity; always a threat and its logic leads to genocide. Racism is virtually synonymous with violence against humans. Always and at the same time racism exudes psychological, social, economic, political and physical violence. I think it is altogether immoral that white theologians and ethicists have devoted so little attention to this paramount moral evil on which this society was built and sustained for centuries. My quarrel with social science is that it has a long history of focusing its attention on measuring the pathological effects of racism and very little on the responses African Americans made and continue to make to effect a better world for themselves and the nation. In fact, the actions of helping to rid the nation of its racism have benefited the moral lives of blacks and whites alike. In fact, blacks have been the primary agents in healing the nation of its greatest moral threat—racism, which Martin Luther King, Jr. said constituted a malignancy in the heart of the nation itself, which, if left unchecked, will destroy the nation.

Most important, my normative criterion for my ethics is the "black Christian tradition" the parenthood of God and the kinship of all peoples." This is the Christian gospel that was institutionalized in the black churches and all societal

The Evasion of Ethics: Peter Paris Feels the Spirituals

the specificity of Christian ethics to a particular material content? Second, what we have portrayed as a virtue in his published books and essays, that is the evasion of ethics, some may consider as a weakness in the sense that he failed to situate ethics as a theological enterprise well connected to scripture, systematic theology, and philosophical conceptual framework.

He may be acquitted of these serious charges if we take into account that at the heart of his work are the two central experiences of all human beings: love and suffering, as Margaret Farley informed us.[56] Add to this list the central goal of social ethics: justice as informed by concern for flourishing life for all human beings. Paris's work, building on the black Christian tradition and the legacy of Martin Luther King Jr., has consistently shown how love (especially love for the neighbor as oneself) is both the appropriate response of those who have and continue to suffer racism and the antidote for poisoned hearts of the perpetrators of racism.[57] Paris's work as we have already noted also points us to justice as giving everyone the real possibility to realize his or her potentialities and to justice as a social expression of love. Love, suffering, and justice are at the heart of the Christian moral life. And his work builds bridges between them.

---

well-being is judged by that ethical norm which is the heart of the gospel for which Jesus lived, proclaimed and died. Because I wanted to take this tradition seriously, I chose to study ethics in a Divinity School rather than a philosophy department. The latter had no concern for religion and religion is an integral part of the African American experience because it provided for them the theological and moral basis for love, justice, compassion, and life itself. (Paris, email message to author, May 12, 2010.)

56. See Keenan, *Catholic Moral Theology*, 197.

57. For example, see Paris, "Christian Way," 125–31, especially 129; Paris, *Social Teaching*, 115–17; Paris, "Meditation on Love," 1–4.

CHAPTER SIX

Literature and Ethics: Learning from Martha Nussbaum

Opening Word

MARTHA NUSSBAUM HELPS US to explore the traditional novelist's attention to the particular and concrete and further enriches our understanding of the vision of the ethical methodology discussed in chapter 1. A crucial part of that vision is sensitivity to the particular problem at hand, and concrete reasons for action as derived from a particular philosophical-theological-ethological perspective of a particular social group. Another important part of this sensitivity is the capacity of agents to move from the particulars to the universal or, more precisely, from the particular to the particular (the particular as an exemplar of the universal). The novelist through attentiveness to particularity in the narrative of characters is often able to invoke in the reader identification with and sympathetic understanding of fictional characters. Nussbaum articulates a procedure by which we can make the connection between the novelist's art and our ethical methodology.

Chapter Introduction

We come to this penultimate chapter of our study with a key question: How can we move from the practical issues of crafting methodology to the practical matters of conscientizing the heart, which is also important for ethical praxis? Can a teacher who instructs students or aspiring ethicists on methodology in the same breath tug at their heart, fire their creative and moral imagination? Is there a way, a method to teach ethics and its methodology that can capture the moral imagination of students and raise their social

Literature and Ethics: Learning from Martha Nussbaum

consciousness? It was Aristotle who taught us long ago that one of the best ways to teach ethics is to use literature, to use it to develop moral imagination. Lionel Trilling states this well: "I spoke of the novel as an especially useful agent of the moral imagination, as the literary form which most directly reveals to us the complexity, the difficulty, and the interest of life in society, and best instructs us in our human variety and contradiction."[1]

Novels, tragic dramas, and other genres have the capacity to help readers identify with fictional characters in ways that show possibilities and potential vulnerabilities for themselves. This kind of empathetic identification is important for good ethical practice in today's diverse and pluralistic communities. Thus, the penultimate chapter of this book addresses literature and ethics. Narrative works of art (such as Greek tragedies, modern novels, drama, poems, and films) are important for developing the human self-understanding critical for embodying certain religious and theological ideals. Good ethical conception and practice often demand that we see things from others' points of view. Great novels, plays, poems, and films are good at helping us to reach empathetic perceptions of particular people and situations by involving our intellect and emotion.

This chapter will explore the connections between literature and ethics: the relationship between creative imagination and moral imagination, the nature of moral attention and moral vision, the role of context-specific judging in ethical decisions. The chapter will help students to deepen and broaden their ethical understanding in ways that involve and give priority to compassion, *similar possibilities and vulnerabilities*, and eudaimonistic judgment, rather than abstract general principles. The chapter relies on the thought of philosopher Martha Nussbaum to help students develop the methodological competence relevant for the use of moral imagination and narrative works of art in ethical reasoning. Overall, using Nussbaum's skills we will learn how to make the vital connections between the novelist's art and our ethical methodology.

The literary imagination or the novelist's art enables the ethicist to pay close attention to particulars in the life of individuals struggling under a social problem and to respond to the person with sympathetic understanding and mercy. Literature invites immersion and critical conversation, nudging the reader to put herself in the place of the character, and thus enabling the reader to see similar possibilities between her own experience and the character. The identification and sympathy of one reader can

---

1. Trilling, *Moral Obligation*, 510.

Methods of Ethical Analysis

also be compared with those of other readers, and with their responses and arguments to the same text. This kind of imagination and response is highly relevant to public reasoning in a democratic society.

When ethics is taught in the classroom through literature, the student acquires important skills for public reasoning. For one, she learns the comparative assessment of situations. The practice of matching her reading of narratives against others, some of which are challenging and others that are affirming, mimics the kind of public discourse in a democratic and pluralistic society. Through this process, she learns the art of critical conversation which must be preceded by immersion, an engagement with the characters to understand their concrete circumstances, hopes, and all that thwarts or supplements their dreams and aspirations.

The question that imposes itself is this: Why do novels serve this purpose while historical and biographical works do not? Aristotle and Nussbaum offer very insightful responses to the query. Aristotle is forthright that literary arts are better sources of philosophy than histories and biographies, which are also narratives. He argues that unlike history, which only shows us "what happened," a literary art shows us what might happen in a human life.[2] Nussbaum's answer to the question flows from this Aristotelian insight:

> Literature focuses on the possible, inviting readers to wonder about themselves. . . . Unlike most historical works [histories and biographies], literary works typically invite their readers to put themselves in the place of people of many different kinds and to take on their experiences. In their mode of address to their imagined reader, they convey the sense that there are links of possibility, at least on a very general level, between characters and the reader. The reader's emotions and imagination are highly active as a result, and it is the nature of this activity, and its relevance for public thinking, that interests me.[3]

Nussbaum's thought as it relates to our project is that the ethicist should draw on the resources of the novelist's art so as to remain capable of *suggnômê*.[4] "The novelist's structure is a structure of *suggnômê*—of the penetration of the life of another into one's own imagination and heart.

---

2. Aristotle, *Poetics*, para 9, 1451a36–1452a10. See also Nussbaum, *Poetic Justice*, 5, 9.

3. Nussbaum, *Poetic Justice*, 5.

4. Nussbaum, *Sex and Justice*, 183.

Literature and Ethics: Learning from Martha Nussbaum

It is a form of imaginative and emotional receptivity in which the reader, following the author's lead, comes to be inhabited by the tangled complexities and struggles of other concrete lives."[5] The public theologian needs this kind of imaginative capability to reason properly about public policy.

In our discussions of the task of ethics and solutions to problems that threaten the moral fabric of society in chapter 1, we talked about searching, imagining, and developing alternatives to ongoing social situations. Indeed, public theology requires that human capability that Mr. Thomas Gradgrind deprecates in Charles Dickens's *Hard Times* as "fancy." But according to Nussbaum, such fancy leads to certain postures of mind, creating the "ability to imagine nonexistent possibilities, to see one thing as another and one thing in another, to endow a perceived form with a complex life."[6]

The novel, by enabling readers to imagine possibilities, thinking about worlds that do not yet exist, is an aid to acknowledging the present world and its limitations and to making choices in it more reflectively. Readers form bonds of identification and sympathy with characters in the novel, taking on their pains, problems, possibilities, and aspirations. There are readers of Ayn Rand's *Atlas Shrugged* who completely identify with the vision of America that John Galt wants to create. Galt wants an American economy that is completely market-and-entrepreneurism driven, one that cuddles innovators, and is supplemented with a very lean government and a fiscal-policy regime that is aimed at maximizing economic growth and innovation and never focused on income redistribution. Some of those readers may have joined the Tea Party as a means of realizing such a vision. In certain segments of the Tea Party, *Atlas Shrugged* is the "Bible" of the movement and Rand is the "goddess" of rationalism, freedom, and pro-growth economic philosophy. On the other hand, there are other readers who reject the visions of Galt and Gradgrind (*Hard Times*) for a more communitarian, humanist social existence. There is no doubt that literature influences reasoning about public policies in the United States.

I share the conviction with Nussbaum that narrative literature has an important contribution to make in public reasoning about ethical issues of our times. Narrative literature helps us to develop the competence to imagine how people who are not like us live and to not resort to a reductive approach to concrete issues. Many students come to seminary or university ethics classes as Mary Dalton in Richard Wright's *Native Son*. Ms. Dalton

5. Ibid., 170.
6. Nussbaum, *Poetic Justice*, 4.

(white upper class liberal) cannot imagine how people are different from her even though poor black folks in Chicago live just ten blocks away from her. Because of this lack of understanding, telling her why black Bigger Thomas acted the way he did "would have involved an explanation of his entire life."[7]

Reading narrative literature will not erase all deficiencies in public reasoning, but will sure help readers to develop an expanded conception of life and the disadvantages suffered by those who are in different class, status, race, and gender from them. This kind of competence or sensitivity is of practical and public value where public theology or social ethics requires us to think in terms of the common good which must of necessity involve persons who are different and distinct from us. How policymakers or ethicists think about the common good is based on some implicit or explicit notion of human nature, of its desires and sociability. What kind of human nature is presupposed in their ethical analyses? Whatever is supposed cannot be taken for granted in our analysis of public policy.

Thus, an important dimension of any ethical methodology is the capacity to model human behavior. Often policymakers and scholars rely on technical models such as economic utilitarianism, patterning processes of inanimate objects, or ideal heavenly scenarios. This they often do to the exclusion of literary imagination. Public discourses and ethical arguments are therefore left bereft of stories, narratives, parables, and mythos that should enrich the search for alternatives to current bad situations. Nussbaum, more than any of the major scholars whose work we have examined and more than anyone else in the American academic scene, deploys storytelling and imaginings as essential ingredients of rational arguments, public debates, and ethical methodology.[8] For her, philosophical discussions of literature, art, and music are part of public policy, business, law, medicine, race relations, and gender relations. Nussbaum uses literature to illumine discussions on the connection between "compassion and mercy, the role of emotions in public judgment, [and] what is involved in imaging the situation of someone different from oneself."[9] In doing this, she is relentless in her effort to inform the reader that narrative, storytelling, and their philosophical analyses are good forms of ethical methodology.

7. Ibid., xiv.
8. Ibid., xiii.
9. Ibid., xiv.

Literary Analysis as Ethical Methodology

Ethical methodology, as I understand it, is a means of interpreting, addressing, and responding to social problems that threaten the social fabric of existence so that we can answer afresh these broad questions: How should human beings live? How should we live together? Literary imagination or the novelist's art is a relevant piece of equipment than can and does provide illumination concerning these questions. The novelist's art—that capacity to present characters or situations in their color and singularity—is very relevant in the work of deliberation, in the kind of practical wisdom and *phantasia* Aristotle insists the ethicist must have.

By not artificially demarcating the moral life ahead of any dialogue into, for instance, how to maximize utility or "what is my moral duty," instead of focusing on moral and non-moral goods that enable individuals and socialities to flourish, we open the ethical methodology to much of what novels present as relevant in understanding how lives hang together. Of course, not every novel or narrative is useful in this respect. According to Nussbaum, ethical analysis is best enriched, enlarged, and endorsed by the content and form, styles and structures, and sense of life of the realist novel.[10] The novelist's attention to particulars and proficient use of imagination to illumine concrete social situations are some of the skills a public theologian needs to have in order to adequately grasp the complex issues of our time. Cultivating imagination, Dickensian "fancy" (as in the *Hard Times*), is one of the pathways to the faculty that grapples with the generation and evaluation of the alternatives that human complexity, non-monolithic sociality, and dynamic social justice require. Such competence must also encompass the capability to balance or accommodate the concrete and the general.

The narrative literature or novel is good at helping us to see how concrete circumstances shape the life of characters. This is often set against general human aspirations, hopes, desires, dreams, and needs. According to Nussbaum, the particular and concrete of narrative literature can promote empathetic reasoning without discarding rule-governed moral reasoning.

> This play back and forth between the general and the concrete is, I claim, built into the very structure of the genre, in its mode of address to its readers. In this way, the novel constructs a paradigm of a style of ethical reasoning that is context-specific without being

---

10. Nussbaum, *Love's Knowledge*, 25–27.

relativistic, in which we get potentially universalizable concrete prescriptions by bringing a general idea of human flourishing to bear on a concrete situation, which we are invited to enter through the imagination. This is a valuable form of public reasoning, both within a single culture and across cultures.[11]

In the hands of Nussbaum, ethical methodology becomes not a procedure of mathematical clarity or certainty, not a kind of explanation of complex human problems as reduced to simplified statements or logic of decision-making. But it is both a release to say what needs to be heard and interpreted about how humans ought to live together and how each person needs to live well, and it is a clarification of the particulars of social existence that inform what human beings are to each other. For her this is what it means for ethical methodology to be both empirical and practical.

> Empirical in that it is based on and responsible to actual human experience.... Practical in that it is conducted by people who are themselves involved in acting and choosing and who see the inquiry as having a bearing on their own practical ends. They do not inquire into a "pure" or detached manner, asking what the truth about ethical value might be as if they were asking for a description of some separately existing Platonic reality. They are looking for something in human lives, something, in fact, that they themselves are going to try to bring about in their lives. What they are asking is not what is the good "out there," but what can we best live by, and live together as social beings? Their results are constrained, and appropriately constrained, by their hopes and fears for themselves, their sense of value, what they think they can live with. This does not mean that inquiry cannot substantially modify their antecedent conception of their "target," specifying goals that were vague before and even convincing them to revise in substantial ways their conception of their goals. But their end is practice, not just theory. And inquiry is valuable because it contributes to practice in two ways: by promoting individual clarification and self-understanding, and by moving individuals toward communal attunement."[12]

It is important to mention that Nussbaum's use of literary imagination as ethical methodology and her analyses of movements in fiction as moments of ethical analysis are anchored to her understanding of the role

---

11. Nussbaum, *Poetic Justice*, 8.
12. Nussbaum, *Love's Knowledge*, 173.

of compassion and mercy in ethical or public reasoning. Compassion and the cultivation of it is key to not only public reasoning, but also issues of social justice in a democratic, pluralistic society. Compassion serves as an important bridge between persons and between persons and community. Compassion is deeply connected to individuals as moral agents in society. Nussbaum's conceptualization of compassion is very illuminating.[13] For her, compassion broadens, educates, and stabilizes elements of concern that we already have. It widens one's own circle of concern. She explains at length that compassion expands the boundaries of the self as it is often set in motion by "painful emotion occasioned by awareness of another person's underserved misfortune."[14] The citizen who feels compassion suffers painful emotion; and now the original pain is doubled due to fellow feeling. Compassion is a process in which the suffering of one citizen is shared by another; hence the doubling. This co-sharing, which can and often does prompt us to treat others justly and humanely, is based on an evaluative judgment of the sufferer's condition.

Though compassion is an emotion, Nussbaum argues that it is rational (based on reasoning), and not driven by irrational sentimentality. She rejects any understanding of emotion that opposes it to reason. The emotion of compassion has a cognitive (thought) structure. It involves the appraisal that the person's suffering is not trivial. It is serious; it matters for the person's flourishing. And thus there is a desire to relieve the person of the suffering. In addition, the person does not deserve it. Implicit in all of this evaluation is the conception of human flourishing and what constitutes a substantive obstacle to it. The evaluation is not all detached and clinical. Either because of shared citizenship, class, race, religion, gender, ethnicity, or sexual orientation, the citizen acknowledges not only some community between herself and the sufferer, but inhabits a sense of similar possibilities and vulnerabilities. The possibilities of the person who experiences suffering are similar to hers and her loved ones. She does not think that she is above suffering and has gotten everything to protect her from all contingencies of life.

In addition to the issue of the *size* of the person's suffering and *non-desert* (undeserved nature of suffering), there is a third element to the cognitive structure of compassion: *eudaimonistic judgment*. The person is part of your scheme or goals and so as such the person's ill condition affects your

13. Nussbaum, "Compassion," 297–353.
14. Nussbaum, *Upheavals in Thought*, 301.

own flourishing. Similar possibility is an epistemological aid to forming eudaimonistic judgment.

Based on this succinct analysis, Nussbaum concludes that compassion is a motivation for helping actions and an essential part of the social justice project of any society. Literature helps in this process of broadening the self. What Nussbaum teaches us is that we cannot afford to ignore the role of emotion in public reasoning. Emotions are built into the very structure of Nussbaum's philosophical-ethical analysis. She gives emotions a carefully demarcated role in her discourse. This writer here is not just talking about the emotions that the beauty, form, style, and brilliance of her work arouses in the careful reader, but how her sophisticated discourse solicits attention for the ideal of full equality, human dignity, and draws the readers' ire against social systems or philosophy that reduce the actual functional capabilities of any human being.

One key impact of Nussbaum's work is that it has redefined the ethical task in the public square. She has shown that the task involves drawing analysts and citizens to see their own possibilities in the lives of others, enabling all of us to acknowledge that we are not self-sufficient, and as human beings we are not accessible only to reason but also to compassionate influence. Plato also recognized that literature could play this role well—all too well. Hence he banned the poets, literary artists from his *Republic* (the ideal city), from the public realm. But for Nussbaum the very ability of literature to arouse emotions, to teach and lead into bonds of identification and sympathy, to see our own incompleteness and vulnerability is what makes it a great tool of both ethical training and analysis. "Literature is in league with emotions. Readers of novels, spectators of dramas, find themselves led by these works to fear, to grief, to pity, to anger, to joy and delight, even to passionate love. Emotions are not just likely responses to the content of many literary works; they are built into their very structure, as ways in which literary forms solicit attention."[15]

To imitate her rhetorical flourish, I will say that emotions are not just likely responses to the often painstaking, insightful, and moving philosophical analyses of Nussbaum, they are built into the very structure and flow, as ways in which ethical discourses solicit attention. Although it is common knowledge that all ethical analyses no matter the methodology that undergirds them want to change human behavior toward a particular goal, the use of literary analysis as ethics by Nussbaum appears to be personally,

---

15. Nussbaum, *Poetic Justice*, 53.

frontally directed at the reader herself, eliciting her desires and giving her a paradigm on how to live her life—or at least emotionally engage with the other as an essential element of her own flourishing. In this way, Nussbaum hopes to bind the moral imagination of the reader to particular, concrete social problems by bringing them close to the (reader's) person's self, giving the reader a first-person reference.

This advantageous feature of Nussbaum's ethical analysis is not about the *content* of her work, although this is very important and worthy of attention, it is about *form*. The very shape of her analyses is subversive of the common attempt to dismiss the ill condition of the other as not affecting one's own flourishing. Indeed, both the content and form of her philosophical-ethical analyses—that is, to say her ethical methodology—constitute an epistemological aid for forming individual eudaimonistic judgment. In her hands, we do not have just an ethical methodology, but a story-formed methodology.

From a Story-Formed Community to Story-Formed Methodology

The other scholars we have studied in the previous chapters also tell stories. But there is a difference between theirs and Nussbaum's. Peter Paris relies on stories reconstructed from archival sources to portray the ethics of African-Americans. Max Stackhouse relies on the grand narratives or sweep of history to anchor his theological ethics of history. Paul Tillich's ethics is the story of the coursing of the ground of being as *substance* through culture. Outside this cohort, we can easily mention Stanley Hauerwas who is well known for his ethics of narrative-formed community.

In all of this, none of them explicitly develops a form of ethical methodology for public discourse that relies on the form, beauty, and style of narrative literature. No doubt Hauerwas often relies on novels (such as *Watership Down* and *The Brothers K*),[16] but I am not aware of his work that developed literary imagination as an essential methodology of ethical discourse in a pluralistic, democratic society. Besides, as Gloria Albrecht argues, though his narrative approach rejects a universal, foundationalist epistemology it often "becomes the new foundation for the assertion of universal truth" or it presses for belief in a single truth.[17] Martha Nussbaum

16. See Hauerwas, *Community of Character*; Hauerwas, *Good Company*.
17. Albrecht, *Character of Our Communities*, 26.

goes beyond narrative ethics (theology) to argue that the very structure of literary works is the format for proper ethical analysis. Hauerwas's work relies on novels to buttress his predetermined ethical treatise, but they are not meaningfully employed to show his readers how they can expand their imaginative capabilities so as to make better choices about the lives they live and make better judgments about the demands of public life upon them.

Nussbaum's work not only teaches us that literary imagination is an ethical methodology, but goes further to elucidate the tripartite method of ethical analysis we set out in chapter 1. Her philosophical analysis of fiction-making imagination embodies in it a form of ethical methodology and a certain sort of moral/political vision—democratic, compassionate, committed to complexity, choice, and qualitative differences. Her work on literary imagination does not merely represent an ethical methodology, "but also enacts it in its structure, in its ways of conversing with its hypothetical reader."[18]

What her work shows is exactly what she likes about narrative literature, especially the novel, as a supreme way of teaching ethics.[19] Thus her ethical methodology is formed and in-formed by the very subject she studies. The convergence has occurred not because she merely wants to stay close to fiction writers, but because like writers of realistic fictions she believes that "life is painting a picture not doing a sum."[20] Fiction writers and Nussbaum approach public reasoning not content to show what has happened, but to show us, as Aristotle believes, "things such as might happen." The genre of novel, according to her, is important for public reasoning because "on account of some general features of its structure, generally constructs empathy and compassion in ways highly relevant to citizenship. Adam Smith was correct when he found in the experience of readership a model of attitudes and emotions of the judicious spectator."[21]

When Nussbaum analyzes a fiction she carefully lays out the viewpoint, the stance, ideology, or behavior that is the source of the problem that is fracturing the social relationship, threatening the moral fabric of society. She will then employ her humanistic viewpoint or Aristotelian framework to define the problem and set the reader up for sourcing or funding

---

18. Nussbaum, *Poetic Justice*, 36.
19. Ibid.
20. Ibid., xix.
21. Ibid., 10.

solutions, suggestions, and responses to the problem. Finally, she will give the reader her opinion on how best to address or rescue the problem.[22]

In *Hard Times*, the problem she identified was the utilitarian, rational choice model that Mr. Gradgrind promotes. Ethics and its methodology in Gradgrind's world are reduced to "some sort of 'sum-ranking' and maximizing procedure, a clear and present solution for any human problem."[23] In the opening scene of the novel Mr. Gradgrind declares: "In this life, we want nothing but facts, sir; nothing but facts." The problem with the economical-mind of Gradgrind is that the utilitarian picture of human beings and of rationality is taken

> not just as a way of writing reports, but as a way of dealing with people in daily encounters; not just as a way of doing economics, but as a way of defining a horse or talking to a child; not just as a way of appearing professionally respectable, but as a commitment that determines the whole content of one's personal and social life.[24]

In this world, all qualitative differences, mystery, and complexity with each life are ignored when public decisions are made, and human beings are added up as data "to weigh and measure any parcel of human nature, and tell you exactly what it comes to."[25]

She identifies the problem, interprets it, and attempts to resolve it all within a tightly argued philosophical framework. The most prominent features of her philosophical framework are given in *Love's Knowledge*. They are (1) "the noncommensurability of valuable things"; (2) "the priority of perceptions" and "priority of the particular"; (3) the "ethical value of emotion" and the imagination; and (4) "the ethical value of uncontrolled happenings."[26]

Let me explain what she means by these features. The first one requires that in doing ethics, we should not place all values on a single scale

---

22. For example, see her analyses of Charles Dickens's *Hard Times*, in her *Poetic Justice*, 13–78; Richard Wright's *Native Son*, in her *Sex and Social Justice*, 154–83; Sophocles's Antigone, "The Antigone: Conflict, Vision, and Simplification" in her *Fragility of Goodness*, 51–82; Euripides's Hecuba, "The Betrayal of Convention: A Reading of Euripides' Hecuba" in her *Fragility of Goodness*, 397–421.

23. Nussbaum, *Poetic Justice*, 23.

24. Ibid., 17.

25. Dickens, *Hard Times*, 11.

26. Nussbaum, *Love's Knowledge*, 36–44.

of ranking or comparison without regard to qualitative distinctions. Values are often incompatible. Second, we must develop the capacity to discern accurately and responsively the salient features of particular situations in making moral judgment. She argues that moralities that are based exclusively on general rules are ethically crude. Third, emotions have a cognitive structure and that practical reasoning must be accompanied with emotion to reach full rational judgment and practical wisdom. Fourth, rules do not enable us to respond well to chance, contingency, and the unexpected that necessarily bedevil all moral life. So the best way to proceed is to understand the particular situation and improvise accordingly.[27]

Now see the way she interprets how Dickens resolves the ethical tension (utility, self-interest as the measure of life that ignores individual particularity) in *Hard Times*. Her interpretation of the resolution fits with her own philosophical framework. It pays to quote her at some length here:

> In its engagement with a general notion of the human being, this novel (like many others) is, I think, while particularistic, not relativistic. That is, it recognizes human needs that transcend boundaries of time, place, class, religion, and ethnicity, and it makes the focus of its moral deliberation the question of their adequate fulfillment. Its criticism of concrete political and social situations relies on a notion of what it is for a human being to flourish, and this notion itself, while extremely general and in need of further specification, is neither local nor sectarian. On the other hand, part of the idea of flourishing is a deep respect for qualitative difference—so the norm enjoins that governments, wherever they are, should attend to citizens in all their concreteness and variety, responding in a sensitive way to historical and personal contingencies. But that is itself a universal injunction and part of a universal picture of humanness. And it is by relying on this universal ideal that the novel, so different from a guidebook or even an anthropological field report, makes readers participants in the lives of people very different from themselves and also [makes readers] critics of the class distinctions that give people similarly constructed an unequal access to flourishing.[28]

---

27. For a good review of *Love's Knowledge*, see Kalin, "Knowing Novels," 135–51.
28. Nussbaum, *Poetic Justice*, 45–46.

Concluding Remarks

Like Nussbaum, none of the other scholars we have examined in this book approaches ethical analysis with skeptical detachment. They neither deem ethical reasoning as akin to formal reasoning in the sciences, nor maintain that the ethicist should be neutral by distancing him or herself from the particulars. But it is only Nussbaum's approach that raises the concern with particulars as a methodological highpoint. By not using an approach that provides a fine-tuned perception of particulars, as the novelist is wont to do, the other scholars portray the ethical as only a collective mode of action, social pattern of events indistinguishable from the political. Nussbaum's ethical methodology not only invites us to engage with broad patterns, but also focuses on individuals and their particular circumstances.

Not that the other scholars lack commitment to the individual, but their variant of the ethical methodology leaves the individual "lives as drops in an undemarcated ocean."[29] Their variant of the methodology is not supple enough or pushed far enough to focus on the social issue (problem, misery) as well as on the individual. Their forms do not promote the habit of the heart and mind that sheds light on an individual shrouded in darkness of poverty or neglect. In Whitman's word their forms to ethical methodology do not let us see "the sun falling around a helpless thing."

Nussbaum has gained this edge over the others because of her deft use of literature. Literary imagination and the novel's ability to focus on the particulars, on individuals and their particular circumstances, is a major aid to ethical judgment. As she puts it:

> I have argued that the experience of novel reading yields a strong commitment to regard each life as individual and separate from other lives. This way of seeing is highly relevant to the questions of well-being. . . . Group hatred and the oppression of groups is very often based on a failure to individualize. Racism, sexism, and many other forms of pernicious prejudice frequently ground themselves in the attribution of negative characteristics to the entire group.[30]

By way of concluding this chapter, let us revisit the ethical methodology as laid out in chapter 1 in the light of what we have learned from Nussbaum. There is something subtle and compelling about the ethical methodology when it is executed according to how we have laid it out in

---

29. Ibid., 21.
30. Ibid., 92.

this book. The methodology works through major alternative positions on how we should live together in the face of a social problem or crisis. These positions are examined and held against one another at three levels: at the stage of analysis of the problem from multiple angles, so as to give full recognition to the nature of the practical situation in its particularity. Next it situates the problem within a philosophical (or theological, ethological) framework, which is likely to fund ways of reasoning about the solution. Finally, there is the search for relevant solutions. The requirement here is that the ethicist should treat approaches to its solution as non-homogenous, and should not arrive at solutions by using a single qualitative or quantitative standard of value in the faulty thinking that all values are commensurable. This requirement, hopefully, will force the ethicist to rigorously engage with other citizens' perspectives on the problem in order to find solutions in the spirit of democratic pluralism. The form or spirit of pluralism—as against totalitarianism—does not go from the particular to the general, but from particular to particular, linking "particulars without dispersing with their particularity."[31]

Indeed, the overall approach or tenor of the ethical methodology taught in this book arguably dovetails into what Nussbaum calls "perceptive equilibrium." This is "an equilibrium in which concrete perceptions 'hang beautifully together,' both with one another and with agent's general principles; an equilibrium that is always ready to reconstitute itself in response to the new."[32] The literary imagination teaches this kind of perception with compelling subtlety and vigor.

---

31. Nussbaum, *Love's Knowledge*, 78.
32. Ibid., 182–83.

Chapter Seven

Conclusion: Ethics of Methodology

THIS BOOK PRESENTS ETHICAL methodology as a *good reading* of any social problem and possible collective mode of action required to transform it. The instructional method teaches the student to study problems and their possible solutions thoroughly by attending to them as particulars of how we should live. Ultimately, to understand ethical methodology as a "good reading" is not to see it as a set of rules applied to social problems and their solutions. It is not a machine for reading or solving problems. Ethical methodology is performed in the good reading, and reading creates the ethical methodology, not the other way round. The proper performance of ethical methodology requires a fine-attuned awareness and attunement to the problems that threaten the social fabric of society. If ethical methodology represents the principles of analysis, then the performance is (in) the understanding that practice will modify the principles under the hammer of "thick" phronesis, practical wisdom. In all of this there is no opposition between theory (as some may read this book) and practice (the actual production of ethical knowledge) because practice and theory in ethical methodology are the same.

As just defined, ethical methodology can exist in a number of different analyses or discourses of social problems, each responding to different problems in different ways, since "good reading" is determined by the particular situation, context, and problem that is being read. Each reading, which is an argument, resists by its presence or representation any arbitrary closing off of the problem by another reading. No one reading can claim to have a determinate meaning. This begs a question: In what sense should a method or reading itself be considered ethical? It is ethical when it exegetes the situation, problem, or the prevailing law of existence to reveal, at least, a path toward living well under justice, approaching justice-to-come with appropriate appeals to human agency or will.

Methods of Ethical Analysis

What is first ethical or where is the ethics? Is it in the methodology, the phenomenological work of identifying the problem and solution, or in the situation? The situation is only understood through the methodology and this representation of the situation is the first ethical. The fundamental ethics here is a method of uncovering ethics—at least as understood in public ethics. The method is the weapon to interrupt, to fracture the situation. Our methodology seeks to break open the situation ("the said") and show the exorbitant overflow of potentiality and possibilities of the particular human sociality. Our struggle is in trying to hear the "saying" amidst the clamor of the said.

What is the point in stating (a) that the ethical as being related to the content of the analysis which points to an alternative beyond the prevailing situation, and (b) the method is itself ethical? We can understand then that both form and content, object and image, objective condition and its representation functions as a *language-work*, expression and materiality (action) of language, to use the terms of Emmanuel Levinas. The connection of these two statements to the ethical—their simultaneous claim to be ethical—is not based on the correspondence of the methodology to the objective condition or comparison between them. The objective condition is the ground of the method existing at all when and wherever it evolves during the continual hammering process of phronesis in the name of what has to happen against the grain of ongoing reality. The fine art of ethical methodology is to weave content and method together even as one moves society forward toward increasing justice and human flourishing.

This movement as we have seen involves a plurality of methods. The multiplicity of methods does not mean that there are no truths, but only techniques for making statements and sites of engagement with the public square in pluralistic societies. Indeed, there is Truth that is empty and as such there is no single place of it that a method can reveal and establish *once and for all*. There are truths, which are compossible and they often point us to the empty category of Truth in the public square without a sacred canopy.

A method cannot name itself as the Truth or the situation, fullness, complete evocation of the Truth. It cannot issue an order for the annihilation of other methods or order that the proponents of other truths *ought not to exist*. This is not the work or operation of a methodology. Method consists in an invitation, a path to livable, co-livable, co-promising truth. Methods point us to truths and truths are compossible. Truth as the central

Conclusion: Ethics of Methodology

category of public philosophy or public policy must explicitly be kept empty in pluralistic societies. Whenever a methodology in social ethics is tempted to go outside its operation to a substantialization of Truth, as the coming to presence of Truth itself it becomes a disaster of thought. The substantialization of Truth "produces terror, just as it produces the ecstasy of the place and the sacredness of the name. It is specifically this knotted, threefold effect— of ecstasy, of sacredness and of terror—that I call *disaster*. At issue is the specific disaster *of thought*. But every empirical disaster originates in a disaster of thought."[1] Often the substantialization of Truth in the public policy of a pluralistic society begins with a person or group claiming, with ecstatic fervor, to precisely name and place the unnameable and un-placeable common good.

Common Good and Ethical Methodology

This book has constructed a proposal for presenting ethical arguments for public policies in a pluralistic society. Its key idea is that any voice that takes differences seriously and wants to speak to the public from its particular stance must learn to speak out of the center of a methodology that is itself serious about pluralism. Such a methodology fractures the singleness or totality of an ongoing social process by putting the system, the speaker, and others into question. Such a methodology, by its acceptance of the right of others to exist, to be heard, and accommodated, establishes pluralism and offers a pluralistic world for our imagination and acceptance. And in a sense it is a mode of comportment and processing of differences in the public square. This kind of methodology teaches and introduces alternatives, new perspectives into ongoing social processes.

I have not specified how any one person or group can appropriate such a methodology. I have only shown how five major American scholars are doing it with the hope that the student will craft his or her version based on insights gained from these scholars and the stimulation of sharpened ethical perception provided by this book. This purposeful inconclusiveness ultimately stems from the philosophy that underlies my understanding of social ethics or public theology.

Before we go into such a philosophical discussion, let us explore some of the possible responses to my constructive proposal. I do this in part to inform students ahead of time on how not to interpret the proposal. There

1. Badiou, *Conditions*, 17; italics in the original.

Methods of Ethical Analysis

are three possible responses to my constructive proposal on methodology. Some students may think that a proper grasp of the ethical methodology presented in chapter 1 and as elaborated upon in the following five chapters transports them into the *real world* of ethical perception or existence. But this reading of methodology as a surface behind which there are real problems and solutions misses the point of my proposal.

The second set of students will maintain that we can only respond to the methodology as a particular representation of problems and solution. There is no objective "behind" of problems that is autonomous and independent from their representation or perception that we can freely access. As per this view, ethical problems are only made clear by the methodology. Social issues are reduced to or are only understood through representation. This is to say the ethical problem is always "interpellated" by methodology. Social problems are always positioned within a field of representation captured by a methodology. Social problems must appear by representation even as they resist and exceed representation within a methodology. This is what interpellation means: even as a problem resists, refuses, and exceeds representation it must be named as that which resists, disrupts representation insofar as it is in a field in which representation has become historically hegemonic.[2]

This second reading is a "thin" reading of the ethical methodology compared with the earlier "thick" reading. Both approaches do not capture the force of the ethical methodology as presented in this book. The power of the ethical methodology as I understand it is neither to transport readers or citizens behind language and observations or to lift up any interpretation of reality as the reality, but is in those places or moments where our senses of reality, self, and relation to ongoing automatism of social processes are "interrupted and put into question" by others and drawn to our responsibility. It is in these places or moments that the ethics of methodology are at its clearest. "These moments of fragmentation are a testimony to the irreducible otherness of the other and to our responsibility."[3]

This is a nice juncture to enter the discussion of the philosophy underpinning the constructive proposal. The unstated thought behind the proposal is a specific notion of the common good and how it relates to differences in the public square and the demands it makes on ethical

---

2. Barber, *On Diaspora*, 95. This paragraph is indebted to Barber's reading of interpellation.

3. Eaglestone, *Ethical Criticism*, 175.

Conclusion: Ethics of Methodology

methodology. I must state from the outset that my interpretation (an immanent understanding) of common good is just one among many and it is possible to propose other interpretations that might work well with the constructive proposal of ethical methodology in this book. In developing one here, my interest is not to enter into the thicket of debates over the "true" conceptuality of common good. It is, more precisely, to further develop our understanding of the ethical methodology I am advancing.

The common good of any society is truly common only when it is in immanent relation with all goods in that society. The existence of a common good in a society means that for each and every one in that community the cause and effect of all goods belong to the same plane.[4] The distinction between goods (such as relations of cause and effect, prior and consequent) is precluded insofar as the common good at the collective level refuses two or multiple categories of goods, two uncommon planes of goods or priority.[5] No groups, classes, or persons stand in relation of transcendence to another even as their positions or preferences are distinguishable. All positions, preferences, and distinctions therefore are preserved in immanent relation. The common good is that good the realization of which demands that every good (of a class, group, race, person) affects others as much as others are affected by it. This is what immanence is about.

> Immanence . . . is a two-way street, even as it maintains the possibility of distinguishing between cause and effect. The fact that effects remain in the cause just as much as the cause remains in itself means that the cause is affected by its effects. It is because of this affection that we say not only that effects are immanent to (or remain in) the cause, but also that the cause is immanent to (or affected) by its effects. The cause is not prior to its effects, for its essence is affected by what it effects; the cause is *constituted* by its effects.[6]

The common good as a concept is a paradigm of immanence. Each individual or group is co-constitutive of each other; no one good is transcendent or transcendental to the other. By definition, there is no transcendent point of reference for the common good itself. It is not conditioned by any

---

4. The concept of common good as developed in this book is indebted to Barber's interpretation of immanence. I have followed his interpretation to creatively fashion a fresh conceptuality of common good on the pivot of immanence.

5. Collective here means a sharing and not a fusion or communion.

6. Barber, *On Diaspora*, 2; italics in the original.

good that transcends it. If one were to exist, the common good will not be the *summun bonum*.

The common good is not even immanent to the open totality of goods (partial goods in comparison with the common good) that permeates the whole community, if the very totality is unaffected by immanent relation. If we are not to deny the immanence of the common good or common good as immanence, we have to accept that the common good is immanent to itself; the common good is common to itself. In the language of philosopher Daniel Colucciello Barber, I would say that common good, then, is "irreducible and autonomous. It cannot be reduced to [a good], for to do so would be to deny the immanence of that [good] to all other [goods]. Concomitantly, we can say that [common good] is autonomous, for the laws of its expression are given by nothing other than this very expression."[7] Thus, common good is not immanent to any totality of goods and "immanent neither to nothing nor to something."[8]

What then is the common good? It is what is expressed by the immanent relationality of all goods. Note that I did not say common good is itself, which will make it transcendent, make its relation to other goods "into something that precedes the enactment or deployment of immanent relation."[9] I have also not stated how this expression could be maintained in a given community, in any pluralistic society, for the expression is never static or done once and for all. The ethical methodology I am advancing in this book is to enable each person or group to diachronically express the common good. The methodology itself must be immanent with the common good; never claim to transcend the common good or fix it as invariant. We are getting ahead of our plan for the unfolding of the argument; let us, therefore, get back to issue of conceptualizing the common good.

The consequence of conceptualizing the common good as a paradigm of immanence is that it becomes impossible to name a good as such, even as the multitude of differences between goods in a pluralistic society demands an appeal to public reason to arbitrate between them. But many scholars name the good as such as "public reason." This is a theoretic approach to "count-as-one" the multiplicity of differences or reasons. The concept of common good, on the contrary, affirms the differential tension between goods but does not offer an abiding theoretical approach to ultimately

7. Ibid., 5.
8. Ibid.
9. Ibid., 6.

Conclusion: Ethics of Methodology

resolve them. But this is not how the concept of public reason works. The tension between the differences provides the impetus for resolution by public reason and as the motor of development for public reason. Public reason works by naming the *inconsistent* differentiality (*inconsistent multiple* in the language of Alan Badiou) of differences as their resolution, a purported straightforward overcoming of differences by positing reason as the *name* (*consistent multiplicity*) of immanence or common good. This move is improper.[10]

Public reason names what is essentially nameless in any public policy formulation in a pluralistic system. What would you say unequivocally is the common good—that good we can all agree upon and it is in immanent relation with all goods in community—except what public reason can name at a particular moment? Public reason, national interest, and *summum bonum* are some of the names we give to what is basically nameless or unnameable; that which is the "substance" of a people's co-existence.[11] That substance is signified to the highest power and invested with maximum meaning and desire when we call it summum bonum or national interest. Public reason names the opposite tendency of expressing it in less powerful ways. None of these names is the proper signification of the common good. They are all contingent names.

Yet we realize that there is a dynamical relation between the names, public reason, and summum bonum. Public reason or summum bonum "imply one another and yet retain an exteriority to one another."[12] They both name a "surplus," or rather the two sides of a surplus. That is, the "surplus thus concerns the mutual displacement that proceeds from immanent relation."[13] Public reason points to the power of common good to exceed the rancor and claimed transcendence of private reasons and goods. More precisely, it articulates the power of immanent common good to exceed the mere givenness or unquestionable acceptance of summum bonum. On one hand, summum bonum exceeds the logical possibility and limitation of public reason, which can be hired as a "whore."

The substance, "being-in-common," common good signified by summum bonum or public reason is an excess that has to be *performed*.

---

10. Ibid., 3–29.

11. Substance is here used in the Spinozan sense, the improper name of what is essentially nameless or un-nameable.

12. Barber, *On Diaspora*, 10.

13. Ibid., 10.

Methods of Ethical Analysis

Common good is not some ahistorical or true essence to which various groups or private (un-common) good would competitively lay claim. It is a performance of being-with, being-in-common of an *inoperative* community, to use the language of Jean-Luc Nancy. The conceptuality of common good being advanced in this book works by putting into play a reciprocal relay between excessive differences and public reason. A major task of an ethicist in a pluralistic society is to "think within the creative possibilities of differences,"[14] with the tension between public reason and differences, between resolution in the name of an *a priori* and open dynamics. The ethical methodology that I am advancing is intent on choreographing this performance at the interplay of public theology and public policy, not to stand as pure philosophical structure to which every expression of the common good must submit.

If we are to remain faithful to the concept of common good developed so far then our methodology cannot have a structure that valorizes or devalorizes the common good. If we give it this structure it will no longer be expressing the common good, but become a philosophical paradigm that conditions the emergence of the common good. For any method to claim primacy over the common good contradicts the *consociality* of a pluralistic stance. Pluralism is an acknowledged *consocial* stance and exercise of separation and interdependencies in social existence. It is a conscious exercise in defining and fostering human flourishing in non-unitary communities. The forms of social existence constructed by pluralistic ethos are meant to be differential rather than identitarian. Difference matters ultimately because pluralism matters. These concerns demand a certain manner of beginning the thinkability of methodology.

Our ethical methodology begins by not imagining that the common good in a policy debate is something already given but obscured by the dust of jostling private goods. It also does not start from the premise that the common good is transcendent and all other goods have a privative relation to it. Rather, the methodology strives to show, starting from a particular position and moving into "interparticularity," how the common good can be immanently expressed by all goods. It aims to reach an agreeable public policy position without reifications of difference or public reason, which will make the common good immanent *to* existing difference or (regnant notion of) public reason. Any reification of public reason or differentiality

---

14. Ibid., xiii.

Conclusion: Ethics of Methodology

of differences makes a (pluralistic) community into a *single thing*. In the words of Jean-Luc Nancy:

> The community that becomes *a single* thing (body, mind, fatherland, Leader ...) necessarily loses the *in* of being-*in*-common. Or, it loses the *with* of the *together* that defines it. It yields its being-together to a being *of* togetherness. The truth of community, on the contrary, resides in the retreat of such a being. Community is made of what retreats from it: the hypostasis of the "common," and its works. The retreat opens, and continues to keep open, this strange being-the-one-with-the-other to which we are exposed.[15]

This retreat is a matter of the political and the promotion of it through methodological form is an "intermattering" of the ethical and the political.[16] Methodology is politics.[17] The question, therefore, is not whether or not a conceptual account of methodology in social ethics can completely transcend politics, but what kind of politics its author and adherents have taken for granted. What then is the nature of politics in pluralistic societies assumed by the conceptual denomination of common good adumbrated in this book? Politics is ultimately about living well, men and women living well in the *common*. The political is "the site where being in common is at stake," and "having access to what is proper to existence, and therefore, of course, to the proper of one's own existence."[18] Thus all political actions (words and deeds) are really about our being-in-common; and what is always at stake in this *in-between* where we are *ex-posed* to one another is the character of possibilities of life. Always and above all this boils down to actualization of potentialities of both individuals and community. And the moral vision that undergirds it is simply, as Aristotle put it: to live best in accordance with the best of ourselves.

From the foregoing it should now be clear that fundamental orientation of the ethical methodology I am advancing in this book is about engendering the creative possibilities in the reciprocal relay between excessive differences and public reason in order to express the common good,

---

15. Nancy, *Inoperative Community*, xxxix; italics in the original.

16. In the Jean-Luc Nancean, the political is about keeping the site of being-in-common open to definition.

17. Methodology at least can be considered as a prosthetic knowledge to shape politics. Politics is "the play of forces and interests engaged in a conflict over the representation and governance of social existence." Christopher Fynsk, foreword in Nancy, *Inoperative Community*, x.

18. Nancy, *Inoperative Community*, x, xxxvii.

being-in-common. This contingent engendering will always be delimited by the conditions of thinkability, undecidability, and the universal precodified horizon of the common good that the engendering immanently relates with. Neither public reason or methodology nor difference can function auto-referentially. Yet the common good is not a form of judgment over any of these; it only provides a mutually constituting relay between them and relays within each of them. It serves as a relay of being-with. The common good should traverse public reason, differences, and the method of articulating them for public policy.

Also, given the immanence that is the common good we cannot argue for the necessity of thinking it prior to its distribution in goods or as the condition of their emergence. We cannot state the common good as the cause of the goods (effects) without insisting that the effects are immanent in the cause. This stance may remind readers of Spinoza's definition of immanent causality, which Gilles Deleuze illuminatingly renders as, "a cause is immanent . . . when its effect is 'immanent' in the cause, rather than emanating from it. What defines an immanent cause is that its effect is in it—in it, of course, as something else, but still being and remaining in it. The effect remains in its cause no less than the cause remains in it."[19]

Without these caveats—refusal to treat the common good as a form of judgment and a transcendent cause—the concept of common good (and the concomitant ethical methodology) will not maintain the "logical possibility of a pluralist orientation."[20] The ethical methodology I am advancing by the conceptual denomination of common good articulates a possibility of immanent existence in non-unitary societies still working out its being-in-common.

In congruence with the concept of common good, the methodology is about becoming rather than being; what can be realized than what has been actualized. It is about how we deal with differences of particularity and the antagonisms they engender in pluralistic societies rather than transcending them and preserving a fully actualized common good, "the hypostasis of the 'common,'" at a plane of reality outside contestation. Thus, our ethical methodology is one way a pluralistic society can perform the possibilities of existence inherent in the common good.

The methodology seeks a symbiotic relation between the integrity of a particular good (stance, moral declaration) and its communication beyond

19. Deleuze, *Expressionism in Philosophy*, 172.
20. Barber, *On Diaspora*, 18.

Conclusion: Ethics of Methodology

the bounds of its owner's discourse. On the account of the conceptual denomination of the common good as immanence there are no encompassing pre-established criteria that must condition the translation (communication). There is no invariant form of the common good invading or rupturing the particular good to turn it into public reason. The translation of a particular moral declaration or private good into public reason or public acceptability is reached not by dismantling of self-enclosed domain of private goods; rather, it is by urging a logic of discontinuity with itself in the encounter with differences that work through the immanent excess of common good.[21] It is by virtue of a recognized difference between a group's particular good as a measure of the common good and the immeasurable immanence of the common good that its starting moral declaration is nuanced at the same time that a relation is maintained with the heretofore particularity. The integrity of the particular stance comes from the group's own sources even as the group turns its discourse toward public reason. As per this principle of the methodology, integrity and discontinuity "are in reciprocal rather than mutually exclusive relation."[22] Accordingly, the ethical methodology or methodological pluralism I am advancing in this book promotes "neither the universal conditioning of the particular nor the particular exception to the universal, but rather the relation between particulars—what might be called the interparticular."[23]

To close our discussion, it is fitting to end with the advice I gave to MDiv students in the introduction: engage rigorously with the six methodological practices of the scholars presented here. I went further to say that this book is about showing different ways of doing ethics, highlighting a kind of methodological pluralism. To reduce or force all the methodological practices into one mold or central view does violence to the premise of the book. Whether this kind of central view is presented as singleness (this preferred method against all others) or totality (this is all there is to a good ethical methodology) rejects all other methodologies as not valid. I urged students to use any of the six methodologies to discover and amplify their own voices without obliterating others or putting their own chosen methodology into the category of "universal truth." These are individual voices that are owned but are not afraid to include echoes of many voices and are open to resonate with others.

21. Ibid., 42–47.
22. Ibid., 54.
23. Ibid., 56.

Bibliography

Albrecht, Gloria H. *The Character of Our Communities: Toward an Ethic of Liberation for the Church*. Nashville, TN: Abingdon, 1995.
Anderson, Ben. "'Transcending Without Transcendence': Utopianism and an Ethos of Hope." *Antipode* 38, no. 4 (2006) 691–710.
Aristotle. *Poetics*. In *The Basic Works of Aristotle*, edited and introduced by Richard Mckeon, 1455–1487. New York: Random, 1941.
Badiou, Alain. *Conditions*. Translated by Steven Corcoran. London: Continuum, 2008.
Baier, Annette C. *A Progress of Sentiments: Reflections on Hume's Treatise*. Cambridge: Harvard University Press, 1991.
Barber, Daniel Colucciello. *On Diaspora: Christianity, Religion, and Secularity*. Eugene, OR: Cascade, 2011.
Bell, Daniel M. *The Economy of Desire: Christianity and Capitalism in a Postmodern World*. Grand Rapids: Baker, 2012.
Bloch, Ernst. *Literary Essays*. Translated by A. Joran et al. Stanford: Stanford University Press, 1998.
Burroughs, Bradley B. "Christianity, Politics, and the Predicament of Evil: A Constructive Ethic of Soulcraft and Statecraft." PhD diss., Emory University, Atlanta, 2012.
Cahill, Lisa Sowle. "Theological Ethics, the Churches, and Global Ethics." *Journal of Religious Ethics* 35, no. 3 (2007) 377–99.
Clayton, Philip. *Minds and Emergence: From Quantum to Consciousness*. Oxford: Oxford University Press, 2004.
Cone, James H. *A Black Theology of Liberation*. Maryknoll, NY: Orbis, 1986.
———. *God of the Oppressed*. New York: Seabury, 1975.
———. "Theology's Great Sin: Silence in the face of White Supremacy." *Black Theology* 2, no. 2 (2004) 139–52.
Copp, David. "The Normativity of Self-Grounded Reason," unpublished manuscript prepared for *Social Philosophy and Policy*, July 2004.
Davie, William. "Hume's General Point of View." *Hume Studies* 24, no. 2 (November 1998) 275–94.
Deleuze, Gilles. *Expressionism in Philosophy*. Translated by Martin Joughin. New York: Zone, 1992.
Dickens, Charles. *Hard Times*. New York: Pocket, 2007.
Dreier, James. "Structures of Normative Theories." *Monist* 76 (1993) 22–40.
Du Bois, W. E. B. *The Soul of Black Folks*. New York: Penguin, 1996.
Eaglestone, Robert. *Ethical Criticism: Reading After Levinas*. Edinburg: Edinburgh University Press, 1997.
Ellis, George F. R. "Physics, Complexity, and Science-Religion Debate." In *The Oxford Handbook of Religion and Science*, edited by Philip Clayton and Zachary Simpson, 752–66. Oxford: Oxford University Press, 2006.

Bibliography

Fisher, James. "Hume's Wide View of the Virtues: An Analysis of His Early Critics." *Hume Studies* 24, no. 2 (November 1998) 295–311.

Goodman, Nelson. "Seven Strictures on Similarity." In *How Classification Works*, edited by Mary Douglas and David Hull, 13–22. Edinburgh: Edinburgh University Press, [1972] 1992.

———. *Ways of Worldmaking*. Indianapolis: Hackett, 1978.

Gregersen, Neils Henrik. "Emergence and Complexity." In *The Oxford Handbook of Religion and Science*, edited by Philip Clayton and Zachary Simpson, 767–83. Oxford: Oxford University Press, 2006.

Hauerwas, Stanley. *A Community of Character: Toward a Constructive Christian Social Ethic*. Notre Dame, IN: University of Notre Dame Press, 1981.

———. *In Good Company: The Church as Polis*. Notre Dame, IN: University of Notre Dame Press, 1995.

———. *The Peaceable Kingdom: A Primer in Christian Ethics*. Notre Dame, IN: University of Notre Dame Press, 1983.

Hegel, Georg Wilhelm Friedrich. *Philosophy of Right*. Translated by T. M. Knox. Oxford: Oxford University Press, 1952.

Honig, Bonnie. *Emergency Politics: Paradox, Law, Democracy*. Princeton: Princeton University Press, 2009.

Hume, David. *Enquiries Concerning the Human Understanding and Concerning the Principles of Morals*. Edited by L. A. Selby-Bigge. Oxford: Clarendon, 1894.

———. "Of the Standard of Taste." In *Essays: Moral, Political, and Literary*, edited by Eugene F. Miller, 226–49. Indianapolis: Liberty, 1985.

———. *A Treatise of Human Nature*. Edited by L. A. Selby-Bigge. Oxford: Clarendon, 1888.

Kalin, Jesse. "Knowing Novels: Nussbaum on Fiction and Moral Theory." *Ethics* 103 (October 1992) 135–51.

Kaufman, Gordon. *An Essay on Theological Method*. 3rd ed. Atlanta: Scholars, 1995.

———. *In Face of Mystery: A Constructive Theology*. Cambridge: Harvard University Press, 1993.

———. *In the Beginning . . . Creativity*. Minneapolis: Fortress, 2004.

———. *Jesus and Creativity*. Minneapolis: Fortress, 2006.

———. "Re-conceiving God and Humanity in Light of Today's Evolutionary-Ecological Consciousness." *Zygon* 36:2 (June 2001) 335–48.

———. "A Religious Interpretation of Emergence: Creativity as God." *Zygon* 42:4 (December 2007): 915–28.

Kauffman, Stuart. "Beyond Reductionism: Reinventing the Sacred." *Zygon* 42:4 (December 2007) 903–14.

Keenan, James F. *A History of Catholic Moral Theology in the Twentieth Century: From Confessing Sins to Liberating Consciences*. New York: Continuum, 2010.

Loder, James E. *The Logic of the Spirit: Human Development in Theological Perspective*. San Francisco: Jossey-Bass, 1998.

Loder, James E., and W. Jim Neidhardt. *The Knight's Move: The Relational Logic of the Spirit in Theology and Science*. Colorado Springs: Helmers and Howard, 1992.

Lyotard, Jean-Francois. *The Postmodern Explained*. Minneapolis: University of Minnesota Press, 1992.

Marx, Karl. "Preface to the First Edition." *Capital*. Vol. 1. Translated by Ben Fowkes. London: Penguin, 1976.

McIntyre, Jane L. "Norms for a Reflective Naturalist: A Review of Annette Baier's A Progress of Sentiments." *Hume Studies* 19, no. 2 (November 1993) 317–23.

Nancy, Jean-Luc. *The Inoperative Community*. Translated by Peter Connor, Lisa Garbus, Michael Holland, and Simona Sawhney. Foreword by Christopher Fynsk. Minneapolis: University of Minnesota Press, 1991.

Noll, Mark A. *God and Race in American Politics: A Short History*. Princeton: Princeton University Press, 2008.

Norton, Anne. "Pentecost: Democratic Sovereignty in Carl Schmitt." *Constellations* 18, no. 3 (2011) 389–402.

Nussbaum, Martha. "Compassion: Tragic Predicaments." In *Upheavals in Thought: The Intelligence of Emotion*, 297–353. Cambridge: Cambridge University Press, 2001.

———. *The Fragility of Goodness: Luck and Ethics in Greek Tragedy and Philosophy*. Cambridge: Cambridge University Press, 2007.

———. *Love's Knowledge: Essays on Philosophy and Literature*. Oxford: Oxford University Press, 1990.

———. *Poetic Justice: The Literary Imagination and Public Life*. Boston: Beacon, 1995.

———. *Sex and Justice*. Oxford: Oxford University Press, 1999.

———. *Upheavals in Thought: The Intelligence of Emotion*. Cambridge: Cambridge University Press, 2001.

Orwell, George. "Reflection on Gandhi." In *A Collection of Essays by George Orwell*, 171–79. New York: Harcourt Brace Jovanovich, 1945.

Paris, Peter. "African-American Religion and Public Life." *Cross Currents* 58, no. 3 (2004) 475–94.

———. "The African and African-American Understanding of our Common Humanity: A Critique of Abraham Kuyper's Anthropology." In *Religion, Pluralism and Public Life: Abraham Kuyper's Legacy for the Twenty-first Century*, edited by Luis E. Lugo, 263–80. Grand Rapids: Eerdmans, 2000.

———. "The Bible and the Black Churches." In *The Bible and Social Reform*, edited by Ernest R. Sandeen, 133–54. Philadelphia: Fortress, 1982.

———. *Black Religious Leaders*. Louisville, KY: Westminster John Knox, 1991.

———. "Catholic Social Teaching and the African-American Struggle for Economic Justice." In *Catholic Social Thought and the New World Order: Building on One Hundred Years*, edited by Oliver F. Williams and John W. Houck, 299–307. Notre Dame, IN: University of Notre Dame Press, 1933.

———. "The Character of Liberation Ethics," In *Struggles for Solidarity: Liberation Theologies in Tension*, edited by Lorine M. Getz and Ruy O. Costa, 133–40. Minneapolis: Fortress, 1992.

———. "The Christian Way through the Black Experience." *Word and World* 6, no. 2 (Spring 1986) 125–131.

———. "Comparing the Public Theologies of James H. Cone and Martin Luther King, Jr." In *Black Faith and Public Talk: Critical Essays on James H. Cone's Black Theology and Black Power*, edited by Dwight N. Hopkins, 218–31. Maryknoll, NY: Orbis, 1999.

———. "David George: Paramount Ancestor of the Black Churches in the United States, Canada and Sierra Leone." *Criterion: A Publication of the Divinity School of the University of Chicago* 35, no. 1 (Winter 1996) 2–9.

———. "Ethics and Politics in Black America: An Introductory Lecture." Harvard Divinity School, Cambridge, MA, Fall 2008.

———. "From Womanist Thought to Womanist Action." *Journal of Feminist Studies in Religion* 9, no. 2 (Spring/Fall 1993) 115–26.

Bibliography

———. "Is it Moral to Make 'Test-Tube Babies'?: A Response." In *The Befuddled Stork: Helping Persons of Faith debate Beginning-of-Life Issues*, edited by Sally B. Geis and Donald E. Messer, 50–56. Nashville, TN: Abingdon, 2000.

———. "Justice and Mercy: The Relation of Societal Norms and Emphatic Feeling." In *Doing Justice to Mercy: Religion, Law, and Criminal Justice*, edited by Jonathan Rothchild, Matthew Myer Boulton, and Kevin Jung, 222–30. Charlottesville: University of Virginia Press, 2007.

———. "The Linguistic Inculturation of the Gospel: The Word of God in the Words of the People." In *Making Room at the Table: An Invitation to Multicultural Worship*, edited by Brian K. Blount and Leonora Tubbs Tisdale, 78–95. Louisville, KY: Westminster John Knox, 2001.

———. "A Meditation on Love." *Princeton Seminary Bulletin* 27, no. 1 (2006) 1–4.

———. "Moral Development for African-American Leadership." In *The Stones that the Builders Rejected: The Development of Ethical Leadership from the Black Tradition*, edited by Walter Earl Fluker, 2–32. Harrisburg, PA: Trinity, 1998.

———. "Overcoming Alienation in Theological Education." In *Shifting Boundaries: Contextual Approaches to the Structure of Theological Education*, edited by Barbara G. Wheeler and Edward Farley, 181–200. Louisville, KY: Westminster John Knox, 1991.

———. "The Problem of Evil in Black Christian Perspective." In *Justice and the Holy: Essays in Honor of Walter Harrelson*, edited by Douglas A. Knight and Peter Paris, 297–309. Atlanta: Scholars, 1989.

———. "Response to Langdon Gilkey's Inaugural Address at the Niebuhr Society, 22 November 2003 in Atlanta." *Political Theology* 5, no. 4 (2004) 475–79.

———. "Review of 'Martin & Malcolm & America: A Dream or a Nightmare' by James H. Cone." *Religious Studies Review* 20, no. 2 (April 1994) 87–90.

———. *The Social Teaching of the Black Churches*. Philadelphia: Fortress, 1985.

———. "The Social World of the Black Church." *Drew Gateway* 52, no. 3 (1983) 1–16.

———. *The Spirituality of African Peoples: The Search for a Common Discourse*. Minneapolis: Fortress, 1995.

———. "The Task of Religious Social Ethics in Light of Black Theology." In *Liberation Ethics: Essays in Religious Social Ethics in Honor of Gibson Winter*, edited by Charles Amjad-Ali and W. Alvin Pitcher, 135–45. Chicago: Center for the Scientific Study of Religion, 1985.

———. "When Feeling Like a Motherless Child." In *Lament: Reclaiming Practices in Pulpit, Pew, and Public Square*, edited by Sally A. Brown and Patrick Miller, 111–20. Louisville, KY: Westminster John Knox, 2005.

Pope John XXIII. *Mater et Magistra* (1961), no. 236. Online: http://www.vatican.va/holy_father/john_xxiii/encyclicals/documents/hf_j-xxiii_enc_15051961_mater_en.html. Accessed February 13, 2009.

Portes, Alejandro. "Social Capital: Its Origin and Applications in Modern Sociology." *Annual Review of Sociology* 24 (1998) 1–24.

Putnam, Robert. "The Prosperous Community: Social Capital and Public Life." *American Prospect* 13 (1993) 35–42.

Radcliffe, Elizabeth S. "Hume on Motivating Sentiments, the General Point of View, and the Inculcation of 'Morality.'" *Hume Studies* 20, no. 1 (April 1994) 37–58.

Reginster, Bernard. "The Will to Power and the Ethics of Creativity." Paper presented at "Nietzsche and Morality Conference," University Center for Human Values. Princeton University, Princeton, 2006.

Bibliography

Rue, Loyal. "Emergence: Nature's Mode of Creativity: A Guide to Thinking about Emergence." *Zygon* 42:4 (December 2007) 829-935.

Sayre-McCord, Geoffrey. "Hume and the Bauhaus Theory of Ethics." *Midwest Studies in Philosophy* 20 (1995) 280-98.

———. "On Why Hume's 'General Point of View' Isn't Ideal—and Shouldn't Be." *Social Philosophy and Policy* 11 (January 1994) 202-28.

Schweiker, William. "Public Theology and the Cosmopolitan Conscience." In *Public Theology for a Global Society: Essays in Honor of Max L. Stackhouse*, edited by Deirdre King Hainsworth and Scott R. Paeth, 123-38. Grand Rapids: Eerdmans, 2010.

Serequeberhan, Tsenay. *Contested Memory: The Icons of the Occidental Tradition*. Trenton, NJ: African World, 2007.

Smith, Michael. *Meta-Ethics*. Unpublished essay, 2005.

Sockness, Brent W. "Looking Behind the Social Teachings: Troeltsch's Methodological Reflections in 'Fundamental Problems of Ethics' (1902)." *The Annual, Society of Christian Ethics*, (1995) 221-46.

Stackhouse, Max L. *Creeds, Society and Human Rights: A Study in Three Cultures*. Grand Rapids: Eerdmans, 1984.

———. "Framing the Global Ethos." Presidential Address presented at The American Theological Society, April 3, 2009.

———. *God and Globalization, Volume 4: Globalization and Grace*. New York: Continuum, 2007.

———. "Introduction: Foundations and Purposes." In *On Moral Business: Classical and Contemporary Resources for Ethics and Economic Life*, edited by Max Stackhouse, Dennis P. McCann, and Shirley J. Roels, with Preston N. Williams, 10-34. Grand Rapids: Eerdmans, 1995.

———. "The Moral Roots of the Corporation." *Theology and Public Policy* 5, no. 1 (Summer 1993) 29-39.

———. "The New Moral Context of Economic Life." *Quarterly Review: A Journal of Theological Resources for Ministry* 2, no. 3 (Fall 2001) 239-53.

———. "Signs of Hope for the World of Business," October 12, 2007. http://www.cardus.ca/comment/article/923/signs-of-hope-for-the-world-of-business/. Accessed September 2, 2010.

———. "Social Theory and Christian Public Morality for the Common Life." In *Christianity and Civil Society*, edited by Rodney L. Petersen, 26-41. Maryknoll, NY: Orbis, 1995.

Stackhouse, Max L., and Dennis P. McCann. "A Postcommunist Manifesto: Pubic Theology after the Collapse of Socialism." In *On Moral Business: Classical and Contemporary Resources for Ethics in Economic Life*, edited by Max L. Stackhouse, Dennis P. McCann, and Shirley J. Roels, with Preston N. Williams, 949-54. Grand Rapids: Eerdmans, 1995.

Stackhouse, Max L., and Peter Paris, eds. *God and Globalization, Volume 1: Religion and the Powers of the Common Life*. Harrisburg, PA: Trinity, 2000.

Stackhouse, Max L., with Diane B. Obenchain, eds. *God and Globalization, Volume 3: Christ and the Dominions of Civilization*. Harrisburg, PA: Trinity, 2002.

Stackhouse, Max L., with Don S. Browning, eds. *God and Globalization, Volume 2: The Spirit and the Modern Authorities*. Harrisburg, PA: Trinity, 2001.

Stout, Jeffrey. *Democracy and Tradition*. Princeton: Princeton University Press, 2004.

Taylor, Mark Lewis. *The Executed Gods: The Way of the Cross in Lockdown America*. Minneapolis: Fortress, 2001.

Bibliography

———. "Paul Tillich's Ethics: Between Politics and Ontology." Unpublished paper, 2006.
———. *Religion, Politics, and the Christian Right: Post 9/11 Powers and American Empire*. Minneapolis: Fortress, 2006.
Tillich, Paul. *Dynamics of Faith*. New York: Harper-Collins, 2001.
———. *Morality and Beyond*. Louisville, KY: Westminster John Knox, 1963.
———. *The Protestant Era*. Chicago: University of Chicago Press, 1948.
———. *Systematic Theology, Volume 1*. Chicago: University of Chicago Press, 1957.
———. *Systematic Theology, Volume III*. Chicago: University of Chicago Press, 1963.
———. *The System of Sciences According to Objects and Methods*. Translated and introduced by Paul Wiebe. London: Associated University Press, 1981.
———. *Theology of Culture*. London: Oxford University Press, 1959.
Trilling, Lionel. *The Moral Obligation to be Intelligent: Selected Essays*. Chicago: Northwestern University Press, 2008.
Ulanowicz, Robert. "Ecology, a Dialog between the Quick and the Dead." *Emergence* 4:1–2 (2002) 34–52.
———. "Ecosystem Dynamics: A Natural Middle." *Theology and Science* 2:2 (2004) 231–53.
———. "Emergence, Naturally!" *Zygon* 42:4 (December 2007) 945–50.
Van Huyssteen, J. Wentzel. *Alone in the World?: Human Consciousness in Science and Theology*. Grand Rapids: Eerdmans, 2006.
Volf, Miroslav. *Exclusion and Embrace: A Theological Exploration of Identity, Otherness, and Reconciliation*. Nashville: Abingdon, 1996.
Wallace, Kathleen. "Hume on Regulating Belief and Moral Sentiments." *Hume Studies* 24, no. 1 (April 2002) 83–111.
Wariboko, Nimi. *The Depth and Destiny of Work: An African Theological Interpretation*. Trenton, NJ: Africa World, 2008.
———. *God and Money: A Theology of Money in a Globalizing World*. Lanham: Lexington, 2008.
Weber, Max. *Economy and Society: An Outline of Interpretative Sociology*. Berkeley: University of California Press, 1978.
———. *Protestant Ethic and the Spirit of Capitalism*. Translated by T. Parson. London: Allen & Unwin, 1930.
West, Cornel. *The American Evasion of Philosophy: A Genealogy of Pragmatism*. Madison: University of Wisconsin Press, 1989.
———. *Prophesy Deliverance: An Afro-American Revolutionary Christianity*. Louisville, KY: Westminster John Knox, 1982.
Williams, Bernard. "Persons, Character and Morality." In *Moral Luck*, 1–19. Cambridge: Cambridge University Press, 1981.
Wolf, Susan. "Above and Below the Line of Duty." *Philosophical Topics* 14, no. 2 (Fall 1986) 131–48.
———. "Happiness and Meaning: Two Aspects of the Good Life." *Social Philosophy and Policy* (1997) 207–25.
———. "Meaning and Morality." *Proceedings of The Aristotelian Society* 1, no. 97 (1997) 299–315.
———. "Moral Saints." *The Journal of Philosophy* 79, no. 8 (August 1982) 419–39.
Yong, Amos. *Theology and Down Syndrome: Reimagining Disability in Late Modernity*. Waco, TX: Baylor University Press, 2007.

Subject Index

A

action, 26, 31, 118, 141
atman, 69
Augustinian tradition, 111
autocatalytic, 89
autonomy, 93, 94, 98, 100
autopoiesis, 82

B

Big Bang, 84, 86
bio-piety, 69
biohistorical, 88-93, 95-96, 100-101
Black churches, 112, 115-117, 121-122
    as surrogate community, 121

C

caste, 66, 67-68
categorical imperative, 29
civil society, 19, 20, 33, 34
    and globalization, 65, 66-70, 72, 76-78
civilization, 14, 35
    and globalization, 63, 64-71, 75, 81, 89-90
color line, 106
common good, 7-9,11-13, 24, 26,130,
    and immanence, 143-151
    and Pentecost, 6-13
common humanity, 44, 48
communal eros, 121
compassion, 17, 127, 130, 133-134, 136
consocial, 148
consociality, 148
consociation, 65, 66
contractarianism, 39, 53, 55
convictional center, 69
corporation, 27, 70, 78, 68
Correlation Method, 114
covenant community, 70
creative destruction, 26

D

Dancing, 9
deep structure, 34
democratic exchange of reason, 42
democratic traditionalism, 53
deontological, 29, 30, 32-33, 48, 57
desire, 8, 9, 97, 131, 147
destructive creativity, 96, 97
disaster of thought, 143
discursive exchange, 38, 48, 57, 59, 69-61

E

ecclesia, 14, 65-68, 70-72, 74, 77-79
eidos, 74
emergence, defined, 81-83
emotion, 17, 127-130, 133-134, 136-138
empathetic perception, 17, 127
empty-category of truth, 142-143
eros, 15, 26, 74, 91, 121, 124
ethical-window, 21
ethology, 29, 32
ethos, 6, 14-16, 28-30, 32-33, 35, 83, 148
    and global civil society, 68-69, 74, 78
eudaimonia, 22, 23, 24, 29

159

Subject Index

eudaimonistic judgment, 17, 127, 133, 134, 135
evolution, 84, 86–87, 89–90, 92
exemplars, 1, 28

F

flowchart, 27, 29, 31–32, 37–39

G

gene pool, 68, 69
geo-piety, 69
global civil society, 4, 14–15, 19, 63–71, 74
globalization, 2, 4, 14–15, 17, 62–79
governmental policy, 35
grace, 29, 33, 67, 71,
ground of being, 80, 81, 85, 90, 94, 99, 135

H

heaven, 99, 100, 105
heteronomy, 93–94
Hinduism, 68–69
hope, 9, 51, 89, 105
human rights, 64, 68–69, 70, 71
humanization, 24, 88, 89, 100
humanness, 24, 100, 138
hypostasis, 149, 150

I

imagination
    creative, 17, 126–127
    literary, 4, 13, 16, 128, 130, 131, 132, 135–136, 139, 140. Also see novelist's art.
    moral, 4, 16–17, 126–127, 135
immanence, 8–9, 11–12, 98, 145–147
inclusiveness, 9, 35, 96, 100
injustice, 15, 107, 109, 110–111, 115, 119, 122

J

Jesus Christ, 6, 7, 111
joy, 9, 114, 134
justification, 41–42, 45, 49, 52–54, 57

K

kairos, 84
Kierkegaardian tragic bind, 88
kinship, 14, 64, 66n4, 116, 124n55,
ktizo, 99
ktizonomous ethics, 95, 99–101
ktizonomy, 98

L

language, 9–12, 144
language-work, 142
liberation theology, 104, 114, 119
love, 9, 58, 96, 100, 125

M

metanarrative, 72, 76
moral fabric, 23, 25, 27, 32, 103–109, 120, 122
moral judgment, 2, 14, 17, 138
    and public reason, 36, 44–45, 47, 48, 50–52
Moralität, 81
multitude, 9–10, 11–12
mystery, 15, 80–81, 87, 90–91, 93–96, 101, 137

N

narrow circle, 41–43, 45, 61
Nieburhrian pragmatist, 118
non-desert, 133
novelist's art, 126–128, 131
novum, 9, 64, 66n4, 83, 94, 113, 118

O

ontological reason, 21
overheads, 90

P

paradox, 12–13, 77–78
payoffs, 30, 33
Pentecost, 6, 8–12
perceptive equilibrium, 2, 140
piety, 34, 44 49, 51
pistis, 65
playing, 9
pluralism, 5–6, 17, 31–34, 52, 53, 59
    and common good, 140, 143, 148, 151
pneuma, 65
point of view of a citizen, 17, 50, 52
political theology, 68, 119
politics, defined, 149
poverty, 77–78, 106, 139
pragmatic-expressivism, 53, 55
praxis, 16, 31, 35, 119, 126
productive creativity, 96, 97
propertyless will, 77
providential, 3, 14, 64, 71
public policy, 3–4, 6–8, 11–14. See also chapter 1
    and common good, 129–130, 143, 147, 148, 150
public square, 2, 4, 8, 11–12, 134, 142–144. See also chapter 2
public theology, 69, 71–72, 74–76, 129, 130, 148
    and methodology 6, 7, 13–14, 19–20, 23, 27, 34, 35

R

racism, 2, 3, 15, See also chapter 5
relationality, 96
resident alien, 6
resistance, 24–25, 26, 107, 124

S

self-organization, 82
sentiments, 17. See also chapter 2
serendipitous creativity, 82, 85, 86, 89, 91–99, 102
Serequeberhanian-Heideggerian reading, 76
similar possibilities, 17, 127, 133
similar vulnerabilities, 17, 127, 133
Sittlichkeit, 81
social capital, 60
spirituals, 16, 105, 123, 124
substantialization of truth, 143
suggnômê, 128
symphony, 38, 50

T

technical reason, 21
teleology, 88, 89
theology of culture, 94
theology of history, 3, 14. See also chapter 3
theonomy, 93, 94, 97–98
thick reading, 144
thin reading, 144
tongues 4, 8, 11
transcendere, 82

U

ultimate concern, 7, 23, 25, 27, 80, 94, 98–99
Unconditional, 15, 80–81, 85, 91, 94–96, 97–101
underivably new, 83
universal common, 63, 65, 67
universal morality, 113
unpredictability, 84
utilitarianism, 39, 41, 53, 55, 130

Subject Index

V

virtue ethics, 55, 111
virtues, 51, 54–55, 64, 94, 107–108, 111, 114
vocation, 70

W

will-to-power, 23

Name Index

Abraham, 67, 87
Acts, 8–9
Albrecht, Gloria, 135
Arendt, Hannah, 113, 114, 117–118,
Aristotle, 16, 106, 111–114, 121, 127–128, 131, 136, 149
Atlas Shrugged, 126
Baier, Annette, 61
Barber, Daniel C., 8n6, 144n2, 145n4, 146,–150,
Bible, 25, 43, 120, 129
Bigger Thomas, 130
Brothers K, 135
Cahill, Lisa Sowle, 7
Clayton, Philip, 84
Cone, James H., 110, 111, 114, 119–120
Corinthians, 9
Dalton, Mary, 129
Deleuze, Gilles, 8, 9, 150
Dewey, James, 115
Dickens, Charles, 129, 138
Du Bois, W. E, B., 16, 106, 115
Galt, John, 129
George, David, 155, 122
Gradgrind, Thomas, 129, 137
Greece, 67
Hard Times, 129, 137, 138
Hauerwas, Stanley, 6–7, 49. 54–56, 112, 135–136
Hegel, G. W. F., 38, 48, 76–78
Holy Spirit, 9, 65
Hume, David, 36–42, 43–53, 55–62
Islam, 68
Jerusalem, 11
Jesus Christ, 6, 7, 111
Kauffman, Stuart, 81
Kaufman, Gordon, 80–101

King, Martin Luther, 104n1, 110–111, 114, 117n31, 122, 124n55, 125,
Kuyper, Abraham, 76, 77
Levinas, Emmanuel, 142
MacIntyre, Alasdair, 54–55, 56
Malcolm X, 104n1, 119, 122
Marx, Karl, 38, 73
Mater et Magistra, 31
Nancy, Jean-Luc, 148–149
Native Son, 129
New Jerusalem, 2, 14, 62–66, 70–75, 78–79
Niebuhr, Reinhold, 113, 114–115, 118
Niebuhr, Richard, 113, 116
Nietzsche, Friedrich, 101
Noll, Mark A., 122
Norton, Anne, 10, 12
Nussbaum, Martha, 1–3, 17, 126–140
Orwell, George, 59
Paris, Peter, 1–3, 15, 16, 25, 103–125, 135
Paul, 9, 65, 66n4
Plato, 111, 116, 134
Pope John XXIII, 31
Postliberal theology, 6
Radical Orthodox, 6
Rand, Ayn, 129
Rawls, John, 42, 47, 56
Reginster, Bernard, 9, 101, 146,
Rorty, Richard, 42, 47, 56
Rousseau, Jean-Jacques, 61
Sayre-McCord, Geoffrey, 44, 51, 53, 55
Serequeberhan, Tsenay, 76n28
Smith, Adam, 136
Sockness, Brent W., 134
Spinoza, 91
Stackhouse, Max, 1–3, 15, 29, 35, 62, 63–79, 135

Name Index

Stout Jeffrey, 1–3, 14, 36–62
Taylor, Mark Lewis, 97, 98
Tea Party, 129
Tillich, Paul, 1–3, 15, 24, 67, 80–97, 113–114
Trilling, Lionel, 16, 127
Troeltsch, Ernst, 34, 113, 114, 116
Ulanowicz, Robert, 89, 90
Watership Down, 135
Weber, Max, 35
West, Cornell, 108, 115
Williams, Bernard, 59
Wolf, Susan, 58, 59
Wright, Richard, 129
Yong, Amos, 32n14

www.ingramcontent.com/pod-product-compliance
Lightning Source LLC
Chambersburg PA
CBHW051935160426
43198CB00013B/2154